This book is dedicated to the children
of Syria, and those who work tirelessly
everyday to make the world a better place.

#BakeFor SYRIA

RECIPE BOOK

Edited by Harry Strawson
Photography by Katie Wilson and Charlotte Hu
Curated and compiled by Lily Vanilli
Design by Sam Thompson
With PR support from Gemma Bell, Gemma Bell and Company
Published by Serena Guen, SUITCASE Media International Ltd
All round support from Clerkenwell Boy
Styling by Lily Vanilli and Safia Shakarchi

For full credits and thank yous please see page 233

CONTENTS

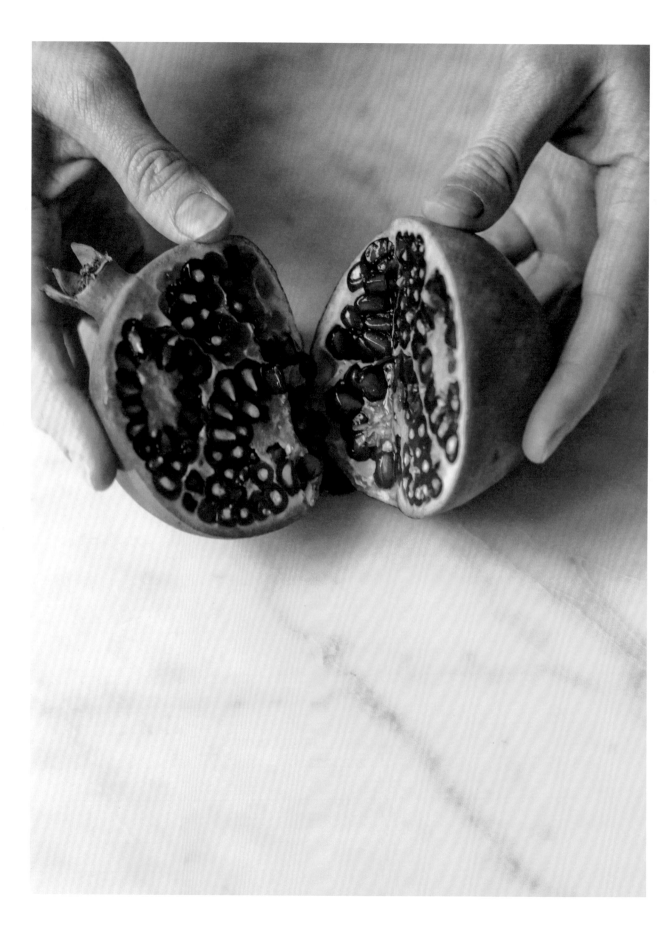

INTRODUCTION

I first heard about the #CookForSyria movement founded by Serena Guen and Clerkenwell Boy when they asked me to contribute a recipe for the original book. Naturally I said yes. The project struck an immediate chord with me, as I know it did with so many others. It has been heartbreaking to watch the crisis in Syria unfold while feeling powerless to help. It is impossible not to ache for the people affected by it and devastating to think of the losses.

Something I admired about the project is that it aims to do more than just raise funds (over £500,000 and counting) for Syrian children displaced by the war. It also celebrates Syrian culture and cuisine, and brings people together to share food and create joy.

In that spirit, last summer (July 2017) I put on the first #BakeForSyria event. The idea was simple: to take the bake sale – one of the most traditional fundraising events – and update it, bringing together some of country's favourite bakeries to celebrate Syrian food and raise money.

I closed down Columbia Road (the street beside my bakery) for the day and we put on an event that assembled some of the best bakeries and bakers in the country, with each creating a dish inspired by Syrian cuisine. Clerkenwell Boy made bunting (ha ha!), Melissa Hemsley DJed and bakers like Bread Ahead, Violet Cakes, Edd Kimber, The Good Egg, Dominique Ansel and Pizza Pilgrims set up stalls. We sold out by lunchtime and raised over £15,000. Later that year, we took over Old Spitalfields Market to put on another event and this time there were queues down the street long before we opened. During that event, the idea for the #BakeForSyria book was born.

As with #CookForSyria, this book is entirely not for profit. It includes recipes and content from some of the world's best bakers, chefs, designers and food photographers, who have come together to create Syrian-inspired dishes celebrating some of their favourite Middle Eastern flavours.

You will find:

- Traditional Syrian and Middle Eastern recipes, generously donated by Syrian families and refugees, some of which have been handed down for generations.

- Modern recipes with a Syrian-inspired twist from award-winning chefs, bakers and food writers from around the world.

- Tips on how to host your very own #BakeForSyria bake sale event.

The recipes in this book and at our events never claim to be a definitive guide to Syrian baking; everything in here is inspired by a love for a particular flavour or dish and intended to be a celebration of it.

I remain in awe of everything #CookForSyria has achieved in such a short amount of time – from a simple idea, a couple of hashtags and a shared love of food. The open hearted generosity of busy people from all over the world – many of whom I have never met – to help make this book and support the children of Syria has been overwhelming.

Lily Vanilli

A MESSAGE FROM SYRIA

Thank you for your generous contribution to the children of Syria. By purchasing this #BakeForSyria recipe book, you are helping these children to overcome their suffering and realise their dreams.

Since the onset of the crisis in Syria in 2011, violence throughout the country has continued, violating the most basic principles of international humanitarian, human and child rights laws, affecting the lives of millions of children and their families.

Indiscriminate attacks on schools and hospitals, using water as a weapon of war, child recruitment and access restrictions on delivering humanitarian assistance to those in need are among the many violations being practiced against children and their families. Unicef has been at the forefront in protecting and advancing the rights of every boy and girl in Syria since the outset of the crisis.

To help these children and their families better cope with their dire situation, and to further enhance their resilience, Unicef provides access to safe water; healthcare and nutrition services; an education and protection from violence, exploitation and abuse.

In Syria, as children face a world that endlessly challenges their aspirations, they continue to demonstrate determination, resilience and hope. I have witnessed this in the dreams of every girl or boy I have met. All children have one wish in common – to continue their education and become the future teachers, architects and physicians who will rebuild a better Syria.

A global commitment to protecting these children's rights can pull their lives back from the brink, and unleash their full potential. By buying this #BakeForSyria recipe book, you will help children who are at greatest need for your support, for which we are deeply grateful. Your generous and valuable support will help us to not leave even one child behind.

Fran Equiza
Unicef Syria Representative

WHY SYRIA?

Syria is one of the most dangerous place to be a child. After seven years of war, children and families in Syria still face violence, displacement, disease and starvation, with nearly 2 million children living in besieged or hard-to-reach areas. Another 2.6 million children are now living in precarious conditions as refugees in neighbouring Turkey, Lebanon, Jordan, Egypt and Iraq.

One in three Syrian children has grown up knowing only crisis. Danger, fear and insecurity has shaped the lives of these young children – and with the conflict in Syria showing no signs of stopping, this number is only going to get higher.

Unicef is working tirelessly to protect Syrian children and give them hope for a happy future, ensuring children have access to life-saving food, clean water and medical care both within Syria and in refugee camps abroad.

Unicef also provides longer term support to help children, young people and families rebuild their lives. Unicef is providing education, psychosocial support and safe spaces for children to play and have some much-needed fun.

In 2017, Unicef helped more than 3 million children enrol in formal education in Syria, and reached more than 770,000 Syrian children with psychosocial support programmes, helping them to cope with the horrors they have experienced. Unicef also provided 6.8 million people with lasting access to water, and vaccinated almost 9 million Syrian children against polio, with the support of partners.

By supporting #BakeForSyria, you can help Unicef reach even more Syrian children. All children deserve a safe home and the chance to learn and play. Unicef will do whatever it takes until every child is safe.

HOW TO GET INVOLVED

HOW TO HOST A #BAKEFORSYRIA BAKE SALE

You can create your very own #BakeForSyria event and raise funds for Unicef while supporting local businesses and doing something for your community.

Here are some tips on how to make it happen.

WHO
Ask your friends, family, colleagues or classmates who are keen on baking and cooking to help with your bake sale. Or, if you wanted to scale it up, you could ask bakeries and chefs from local restaurants in your area to participate in a bigger event. It's good to have a balance of sweet, savoury and hot food at the event, so there's something for everyone. Think about variety; it could be ice cream or a savoury pastry. We asked all the participants at our Columbia Road #BakeForSyria event to create at least one Syrian-inspired dish – but don't feel you have to do this too!

SPACE
You could host your event at home, school or the office. If you're scaling up, ask the council if you can take over space in your neighbourhood for the day of the event, such as a local market street or a park. If it's summer, you can try and get lucky with the weather and host it outdoors, though it's worth having a backup plan in case it rains. At the first #BakeForSyria the weather was fine until around two o'clock when the skies opened – fortunately we had all but sold out by then, and everyone was having so much fun, we hardly noticed.

SET UP
You can go a long way with trestle tables and tablecloths, but we hired little candy striped market stalls from an events company for the Columbia Road event. Each business or baker will probably want to put their own stamp on their stall, so encourage them to bring signage, linens, plants and cake stands, or whatever they choose to decorate the space with, as well as practical things like a cash box and napkins. Find out in advance if anyone needs power and make sure they have access. Also be sure to clearly label ingredients and how food was prepared in case of any guest allergies or dietary restrictions.

PROMOTING IT
Use the #BakeForSyria hashtag on Instagram, Twitter and Facebook and ask all the people involved to help spread the word to their friends, family and fans. You can print posters and flyers too – resources are available on our website.

SHARE THE LOVE
@CookForSyria
#BakeForSyria
@NextGenLondon
@UNICEF_UK

MONEY RAISED
How you organise the donations might vary case by case (for instance, if you have a sponsor to help with covering costs), but we think the simplest arrangement is for vendors to donate £1 of every sale. You can then collate this and make the donation in bulk to Unicef via NEXTGen London – visit our website for details on how to give.

Xx Lily

For more information,
visit CookForSyria.com/Bake-For-Syria
or email hello@cookforsyria.com

STORE CUPBOARD ESSENTIALS

ALEPPO CHILLI

Hailing from the Silk Road spice route, these rich red peppers are both gentle and fragrant. They are dried, de-seeded and ground into coarse flakes that add a mild heat to any dish.

BAHARAT

Baharat is a popular, all-purpose spice used across the Middle East. If you can't buy it, then it's quite easy to make your own to taste using allspice, black peppercorns, cinnamon, coriander seeds, cloves, nutmeg and paprika. A little goes a long way.

CARDAMOM

Has an exotic, rich aromatic that betrays its status as the world's third most expensive spice. It adds a depth to any dish – sweet or savoury and goes well with everything from coconut to banana and chocolate.

CHICKPEAS

A versatile ingredient that can be used in dips (such as hummus), snacks (such as falafel) and larger dishes (such as fatteh).

COCONUT

Used in sweet and savoury dishes, the coconut can be used to balance both sweetness and spice and add moisture and a density of texture.

DATES

Perfect in both sweet and savoury dishes, we especially love medjool dates (often described as "the king of dates"). They are large and soft in texture, with a beautiful caramel and honey flavour profile. Date syrup is often used in dishes to add a layer of sweetness.

FLATBREAD

Flatbreads are an essential part of any Syrian meal and are great for dipping into hummus, soups and stews, or when used in fattoush (bread salad). Many of the #BakeForSyria recipe book contributors have provided recipes for their favourite flatbread.

JASMINE

The unofficial flower of Syria, used in teas and easily infused into rice or cakes, jasmine has the most intoxicating, enigmatic aroma and flavour.

KATAIFI

A kind of shredded filo pastry, with a threadlike dough plays a traditional role in Middle Eastern confectionery and treats, and makes a good nest for dessert ingredients.

LABNEH

A fresh cheese made from yoghurt that has been strained to remove its whey, resulting in a thicker consistency. Perfect for spreading on flatbread, or rolled into a ball and dipped in various herbs and spices.

MINT

Dried mint is used in many recipes and marinades.

ORANGE BLOSSOM WATER

Made from the distilled blossoms of orange trees, this intense and fragrant liquid can be used in syrups, cakes, rice puddings and baklavas.

PISTACHIO

Said to have been native to Syria as far back as 6750 BC, pistachios are one of the most well loved nuts around the world. Their vibrant green colour and exotic flavour mean they add elegance and depth to any dish.

POMEGRANATE

The jewel-like, ruby-coloured flesh of pomegranates can transform everyday dishes into something special.

ROSE WATER

One of the most famous flowers in the world, the Damask rose has been used for centuries in the Middle East and beyond to flavour desserts and sweet treats.

SUMAC

Sumac is a rich, burgundy-coloured spice with a distinctive lemony flavour. It tastes great with salads and grilled meats, and is also delicious sprinkled over hummus.

TAHINI

Tahini is a paste made from ground sesame seeds. It has a distinctive taste and is used in dips, sauces and to complement savoury dishes – but also works well with cakes and desserts.

TURMERIC

This vibrant kindred of the ginger family gives a powerful deep yellow orange colour to everything it touches, and a warm, bitter, peppery flavour along with an earthy aroma. It is also said to have multiple health benefits.

YOGHURT

An essential and versatile ingredient used for mezze, salads, main courses and desserts.

ZA'ATAR

Za'atar is an intensely aromatic spice blend traditionally made with dried herbs such as marjoram or thyme (the Arabic word za'atar also means thyme). It is commonly used on flatbreads or to flavour meat and vegetable dishes.

I. CAKES

—

JASMINE AND DAMASK ROSE CAKE

Donated by Lily Vanilli
@lily_vanilli_cake

"I'm grateful for the opportunity #CookForSyria and now #BakeForSyria has given me to do something to help those affected by a humanitarian crisis which has been heartbreaking to watch unfold while feeling powerless to help. Serena and Clerkenwell Boy came up with a way to turn a lot of people's good will into something that can actually help others, and the project not only raises significant money to help children affected by the war in Syria but endeavours to celebrate Syrian cuisine and culture and create joy."

Serves 10

250g soft, room temperature butter

2.5 tsp loose leaf jasmine tea

190g caster sugar

3 eggs

125ml whole milk

2 tsp baking powder

190g plain flour

fresh flowers of your choice for decoration

I use a lot of flowers in my cakes and Syria is known for its beautiful Damask roses as well as its national flower jasmine, so I wanted to create a cake for this book that is a celebration of Syrian blooms. This one is infused with jasmine for its flavour, and decorated with trailing jasmine and roses for their beauty (note, the oil of the Damask rose has a lovely flavour too).

The Greek poet Sappho said of the Damask rose, "It is the pride of plants, and queen of flowers".

Over a low heat, melt the jasmine leaves with 100g of the butter, let it bubble very gently for three mins then take it off the heat and stir. Leave it to cool and steep at room temperature for at least an hour.

Now press the cooled butter through a sieve to remove the tea leaves and beat all of the butter, together with the sugar until it's light and fluffy.

Scrape down the bowl, add the eggs and mix to combine evenly.

In a separate bowl, combine the flour and baking powder evenly, then add this to the mix, beating until combined, followed by the milk, then beat everything to just combine to a smooth and even batter.

I used three 15cm cake pans for this cake but you could equally bake this mix in two 18 or 20cm pans for a different shaped cake.

Just grease your pans well, tip the batter in, spread evenly and bake for around 20-25 mins or until a toothpick inserted into the centre of the cake comes out clean.

Use any buttercream recipe you like to sandwich between the layers and then ice all over for a smooth finish, and decorate with the flowers.

There is a recipe for my buttercream and a guide to icing a layer cake on my website if you want some extra tips.

Finish with fresh flowers.

Photography by @CharlotteHuCo
Styling by @lily_vanilli_cake
Portait by @alicewhitby

CAKES

MINI LOVE CAKES

Donated by Katherine Sabbath
@katherine_sabbath

"Any cause aimed at increasing awareness of the plight of children in war-torn countries such as Syria is one that, as global citizens, we need to support. I am passionate about this initiative directed by Unicef, which helps raise funds to protect the children of Syria. I truly believe that even the smallest acts of cooking, sharing recipes and using the power of social media can help make a positive contribution."

Spiced caramel loaves

200g unsalted butter, chopped into chunks

200g good quality white chocolate, chopped

150g (3/4 cup, firmly packed) dark brown sugar

250ml (1 cup) hot water

2 tbsp honey

2 tsp vanilla extract

2 large, free-range eggs, at room temperature

150g (1 cup) self-raising flour

225g (1 1/2 cups) almond meal

2 tsp cinnamon

1 tsp ground ginger

1 tsp ground cardamom

Rose cream cheese

500g cream cheese, softened

100g butter, softened

125g icing sugar (1 cup), sifted

1/2 tsp rose water

2 tsp lemon juice

3-4 drops pink food colouring or natural colouring extract

150ml thickened cream, whipped

Assembly

1 cup crushed pistachios

4 cubes of Turkish Delight, chopped into smaller squares

3 fresh figs, sliced into wedges

edible gold dust (optional - available at cake decorating supplies stores)

edible gold leaf (optional - available at cake decorating supplies stores)

Filled with classic aromatic flavours of cinnamon, ginger, and cardamom, it is almost impossible to resist these beautiful mini love cakes. The spiced caramel and almond mini loaves are deliciously sticky, and adorned with sweet, plump figs and jewel-like cubes of Turkish Delight, these mini cakes are sure to win hearts!

Mini loaves
Makes 8
Preheat oven to 160°C fan.

Prepare a mini loaf pan.

Place butter, chocolate, sugar, water, honey and vanilla in a heavy-based saucepan. Stir over medium-low heat until chocolate melts completely and your mixture is smooth. Set aside to cool.

Next, add the eggs, one at a time and beat well with a mixer.

Combine sifted flour and spices with your white chocolate mixture, then fold in almond meal evenly.

Fill each cavity to 3/4 full. Bake for 30 mins until or until a wooden skewer comes out almost clean. Leave to cool completely.

Rose cream cheese
Whip together cream cheese, butter, icing sugar, rose water, and lemon juice until pale and fluffy.

Add food colouring as desired.

Gently fold in whipped cream until combined and set aside until needed.

TIP: If your filling is too soft to pipe neatly, rest it in the fridge to firm up.

Assembly
Using a piping bag with a star-tipped nozzle, pipe rose cream cheese onto each loaf. Add crushed pistachios, Turkish Delight cubes, and sliced fresh figs.

Photography by @nikkito
Portrait by @nikkito

TAHINI & YOGHURT BUNDT CAKE WITH POMEGRANATE & ROSE WATER DRIZZLE, PISTACHIO DUST

Donated by Jamie Oliver
@jamieoliver

"I want to big up Clerkenwell Boy and all the incredible chefs supporting this cause. In a world where it's hard to see the wood for the trees, it can be difficult to know which issues and stories to prioritise. #CookForSyria makes it easy for people to get involved and for the public to offer support. It's an honour to be a part of it."

Serves 18

For the dough

375g unsalted butter (at room temperature), plus extra for greasing

375g golden caster sugar

375g self-raising flour

150g natural yoghurt

2 tablespoons tahini

6 large free-range eggs

2 lemons

1 orange

150g shelled unsalted pistachios

For the drizzle

1 pomegranate

1 lime

½ teaspoon rose water

300g icing sugar

It's an absolute pleasure to take some incredible Syrian flavours and blend them with some of the emotions of my Nan's baking. This beautiful cake can be served at tea, at a picnic, or even as a delicious dessert with ice cream or hot custard. Feel free to experiment with cupcakes as well – they'll take about 20 mins to bake.

Preheat the oven to 180ºC. Generously grease a 2-litre bundt tin with butter.

Place the sugar, flour, butter, yoghurt and tahini into a food processor. Crack in the eggs, squeeze in all the citrus juice and blitz until smooth.

Pour the mixture into the bundt tin, scraping it out of the processor with a spatula, then give the tin a jiggle to level out the mixture. Bake for 50 to 55 mins, or until golden and an inserted skewer comes out clean.

Leave the cake to cool in the tin for 5 mins, then turn out onto a wire rack and leave to cool completely.

To make the amazing drizzle, halve the pomegranate and squeeze 30ml of juice through a sieve into a jug, then squeeze in 30ml of lime juice. Pour into a bowl with the rose water, then stir in the icing sugar to give you a thick drizzling consistency.

Smash up the pistachios in a pestle and mortar into a mix of random small chunks and lovely dust.

Pour the drizzle over the cooled cake, letting it drip down the sides. Slice, and serve with a sprinkling of pistachio dust.

Photography by @jamieoliver Jamie Oliver Enterprises Limited
Styling by Jamie Oliver Enterprises Limited
Portrait by @matt_russell

CAKES

SPICED PEAR CAKE WITH TAHINI BUTTERCREAM

Donated by Rosie Birkett
@rosiefoodie

"At one of the #CookForSyria pop-ups I spoke to my friend, Syrian chef and restaurateur Imad Alarnab about how important feasting and sharing food is in Syria. It was heartbreaking to hear how his restaurants in Damascus had been lost to the war. Imad insisted that it was a small loss compared to what others had suffered and that is just one of the reasons why I support #BakeForSyria – so that we might raise awareness and funds for the next generation of Syrian children who desperately need our help."

For the cake

4 williams pears, grated over a sieve, reserving the pear juice

1 williams pear, peeled, cored and chopped

2 medjool dates, chopped

2cm piece of ginger, grated

360g self raising flour

15g rye flour

1 tsp ground ginger

1/2 tsp turmeric

1/2 tsp nutmeg, freshly grated

1 tsp cardamom, freshly ground

1 tsp cinnamon

1 tsp baking powder

1 tsp sea salt

4 eggs

200g granulated sugar

150g brown sugar, sieved

150ml rapeseed or vegetable oil

120g natural yoghurt

For the pear salted caramel

50ml pear juice

150ml pear cider caramel

100g brown sugar

50g unsalted butter

1 tbsp double cream

½ tsp sea Salt

For the icing

4 egg whites

250g sugar

250g butter, room temperature

2 tbsp tahini

1 tbsp vanilla bean paste

For the garnish

pear, figs, rosemary, buckwheat.

I originally created a version of this recipe for a feature I did on food for sharing. It's a real celebration cake full of warming spices, sweet pear and medjool dates, and iced with a fluffy, silky tahini buttercream. I thought it would be perfect for this book, since both communal feasting and tahini are central to Syrian cuisine.

Serves 15 - 20

Preheat the oven to 175°C and prepare three 20cm cake tins.

Sieve the flours, baking powder, salt into a bowl with the spices and stir to combine. In a stand mixer, vigorously beat the sugar and eggs for 3 mins, until thick, pale and frothy. Slowly pour in the oil in a steady stream. Turn the speed down to 6 and add two spoonfuls of flour at a time, alternating with the yoghurt, until it's all incorporated. Then mix in the grated pear for no longer than 20 seconds. Divide between the tins and bake for 24-26 mins, until a skewer inserted comes out dry.

To make the buttercream, put the sugar and egg whites into the bowl of a stand mixer and mix with the whisk attachment. Create a bain-marie, with a large pan with an inch or two of boiling water and whisk the egg whites and sugar over the heat until it's too hot to touch. Re-insert it into the stand mixer and beat with the whisk until soft peaks, and the bowl is back at room temperature. Swap in the paddle attachment and start to add in the butter, a spoonful at a time, until all incorporated, then add in the tahini and a pinch of salt and whisk until you have a light, fluffy icing.

Place the bottom layer of sponge on your platter or cake stand and top with a thin layer of the buttercream. Scatter over a third of the chopped pear and dates and lay on the next layer of sponge. Repeat with the next two layers, then ice the cake, doing a thin crumb coating and refrigerating for 20 mins or so and then do the top coat.

To make the salted caramel, place the pear cider and pear juice in a pan and reduce to about 50ml. Add the butter and sugar and whisk until you have a smooth caramel, then add the cream and whisk until smooth. Season with salt to your taste – I'd go for a generous pinch, it should be fruity, sharp and not overly salty but just enough to pique the caramel.

Allow to cool slightly – but you need it slightly warmer than room temp to pour it. Pour it onto the top of the cake and allow to drip over the sides. Use a stepped spatula to spread it out evenly. Garnish with toasted buckwheat, rosemary and the dehydrated pear.

Photography by @KatieWilsonFoto
Styling by @dearsafia
Portrait by @helencathcart

CAKES

TAHINI, HONEY AND CINNAMON BAKED CHEESECAKE

Donated by Felicity Spector
@felicityspector

"I got involved in #CookForSyria as soon as it was first conceived. It's a truly wonderful initiative involving all sorts of people in hospitality and food. I really appreciated all the hard work and generosity which has made it such a success. The world must not forget the millions of Syrians whose lives have been devastated by war, who have lost everything and left all they know behind. Food and the sharing of food can bring us together: it is something, it is inspiring."

200g digestive biscuits

200g speculoos biscuits

Approx. 100g butter, melted

800g full-fat cream cheese (at room temperature)

2 large eggs (at room temperature)

200g golden caster sugar

60g runny honey

50g cornflour

250ml whipping cream

2 tbsp tahini

1 tsp cinnamon

1 tsp vanilla extract

figs and crushed pistachio to serve (optional)

I'm always asked about my favourite dessert. It's impossible to choose, of course, but a proper baked cheesecake would be up there. It reminds me of so much: of my dad who loved it; of living in New York. I wanted to create a version which used the Middle Eastern flavours I love - the richness of tahini, warm cinnamon and fragrant honey. These are the flavours which bring food alive, which recall the dry heat of the Jordan valley, the noise of the souk, the shared platters of food passed around a table of friends, sitting out in the open under the orange trees, still warm as dusk turns to night.

Serves 12-15

Preheat oven to 130°C and lightly grease a 25cm springform baking tin and line the base with parchment paper.

For the base
Crush the biscuits in a food processor or bash with a rolling pin inside a sealed freezer bag until they resemble fine sand.

Add the melted butter, mixing thoroughly so all the crumbs are coated. Press a small amount into a ball: if it comes together and then crumbles when you touch it, that's the right amount of butter.

Press the base into the prepared tin with the back of a spoon so that it's level, and put in the fridge for 30 mins while you make the topping.

Put the cream cheese into a stand mixer with the paddle attachment and add the sugar: mix until smooth and the sugar has melted. Add the honey and mix again to combine. Add the eggs, one at a time, until thoroughly incorporated – making sure you scrape down the sides of the bowl a couple of times. Sift in the cornflour and stir through, then add the tahini, the whipping cream, the vanilla and cinnamon and mix again to combine.

Pour the topping on top of the chilled biscuit base, and bake on the middle shelf of the oven for approx 1 hr 20 mins – or until the top no longer looks wet and shiny and the centre jiggles just a bit when you gently shake the tin.

Turn off the oven, prop open the door with a wooden spoon and leave the cheesecake to cool inside for an hour to prevent cracking, then cool completely on a wire rack before covering the tin with foil and refrigerating for 8 hours – or overnight.

Release the springform tin to umould and slide carefully onto a plate, sliding the greaseproof paper from under the base before serving.

Photography by @CharlotteHuCo
Styling by @lily_vanilli_cake

CHICKPEA BANANA BREAD WITH DATES, CINNAMON AND ALEPPO PEPPER GF, DF, V

Donated by Jasmine Hemsley
@jasminehemsley

"It's an honour to have been involved with #CookForSyria and I am immensely proud of what has been achieved by all those who took part. Using Syrian produce is a brilliant way to honour and support the country, and as an avid baker (and someone with a sweet tooth!) I jumped at the opportunity to get involved in #BakeForSyria."

Serves 10

4 medium ripe bananas, mashed - 400g plus one extra medium banana, chopped

2 tbs dark jaggery or maple syrup (adjust sweetness to your liking)

2 tsp vanilla extract

¼ cup water

4tbsp olive oil

1½ cups/180g chickpea flour (aka garbanzo/besan/gram flour)

¼cup/25g ground flax

2 tsp baking powder

1.5 tbs cinnamon

1/4 tsp salt

½ - 2 tsp Aleppo pepper, depending on strength (or use 1tsp sweet or plain paprika and 3/4tsp cayenne)

4 medjool dates or 6 dried dates - chopped into chunks

½ cup/50g walnuts pieces or pistachios

I love banana bread! I've adapted the banana bread recipe in my Ayurveda-inspired cookbook East by West with Syrian ingredients and flavours to create a bread which is tasty, good for you and has a warming spiced finish. I've used classic Syrian ingredients including chickpeas for a protein-rich base; cinnamon for a warm, spicy taste; chunks of dates that go chewy in the oven; and nutty olive oil and walnuts. I also added Aleppo pepper for a fragrant, sweet and salty kick of chilli. It's an easy recipe so great for everyone - and if the kids are not crazy about hot spices then you can substitute the chilli for a handful of chocolate chips!

Preheat the oven to Fan 180C

Blend everything (except the dates, nuts and the extra chopped banana) in a food processor, then continue to step 3 or follow the instructions below:

Mash 4 of the bananas with the jaggery, vanilla, water and olive oil in one bowl. Mix the chickpea flour, flax, baking powder, cinnamon, nutmeg, sea salt and Aleppo pepper together in another bowl. Mix everything together until well combined.

Transfer the mixture to a 750g (11/2 lb) or 1kg loaf tin lined with baking parchment. Mix in the chopped dates, chopped banana and walnut pieces/pistachios by hand (I use a chopstick to quickly stir them in and distribute), reserving some of the dates for the top.

Top with the remaining chopped dates, push them in slightly and bake in the middle of the oven for 30-35 minutes, until the bread is firm-ish to the touch. Allow to cool before slicing (it will carry on cooking), then serve with butter or extra virgin olive oil.

Delicious warmed in the oven or grilled

NB - don't worry if the bread is not cooked through when tested with a skewer - just check that it's firm to touch and then as it cools it will continue cooking

Tip: To make muffins, bake in a lined muffin tin for 15-20 minutes.

DESSERTS

Photography by @nickhopper_galacticman
Portrait by Nick Hopper

TURMERIC SHREDDED COCONUT CAKE

Donated by Lily Vanilli
@lily_vanilli_cake

"I'm grateful for the opportunity #CookForSyria and now #BakeForSyria has given me to do something to help those affected by a humanitarian crisis which has been heartbreaking to watch unfold while feeling powerless to help. Serena and Clerkenwell Boy came up with a way to turn a lot of people's good will into something that can actually help others, and the project not only raises significant money to help children affected by the war in Syria but endeavours to celebrate Syrian cuisine and culture and create joy."

Serves 8-10

For the cake
330g plain flour

320g caster sugar

1½ tbsp baking powder

Pinch of salt

175g unsalted butter, at room temperature

3 eggs

190ml whole milk

1½ tsp grated fresh turmeric

3 x 18cm cake tins - greased and lined

To decorate
100g shredded or thread coconut

one batch of buttercream of your choice

(see my website for a recipe if you need one)

For the caramel almond crunch
50g butter

75g granulated sugar

3 tablespoons honey

2 tablespoons double cream

Pinch of Maldon sea salt

1 1/2 handfuls toasted, flaked almonds

This is a great cake to make for a party, it looks like it's ready to burst with all the shredded coconut and caramel almonds. You can skip the almonds if you want a simpler cake – it's still delicious – but I think it's worth the extra effort.

For the cake
Preheat oven to 180°C.

In a bowl, whisk together the dry ingredients and the turmeric. Beat in the butter until it is incorporated and the mixture appears to be evenly coated and looks like a fine crumble mix – about 2-3 mins on medium speed.

Add the eggs and beat, first on medium, then on high, just until incorporated.

Add the milk and beat, on medium and then on high, for 2-3 mins until the mixture is smooth and combined; it will appear a bit lighter in colour.

Divide the mixture between the prepared cake tins and level out to the edges. Bake in the oven for 25-30 mins, or until a toothpick inserted into the centre comes out clean. Remove from the oven and leave to cool in the tins for 10 mins before turning out on to a wire rack to cool completely.

For the almond crunch
Put the butter, sugar, honey, cream, and salt in a saucepan over medium heat, stirring to melt the butter.

Bring to a simmer, stirring often, and let boil for 3 mins or until the mixture turns a light beige colour.

Now stir in the almonds, the mixture will be very thick and sticky. Place on a lined baking sheet and bake for around 15 mins or until just golden brown. Leave to cool.

To assemble
Place one cooled cake layer onto your plate, spread on some buttercream, followed by coconut and then the almond. Repeat all the way to the top.

Photography by @CharlotteHuCo
Styling by @lily_vanilli_cakei
Portait by Alice Whitby

BAKED ORANGE BLOSSOM CHEESECAKE

Donated by Jooles O'Sullivan of The Good Egg
@thegoodegg_

"So many innocent people have lost their lives or their loved ones in this devastating conflict. #BakeForSyria is a fantastic way not only of raising awareness and vital funds for the plight of the Syrian people, but also celebrating the country and its cuisine's bold flavours, which continue to influence and inspire what I make in the kitchen."

For the pumpkin
1 pumpkin/squash (400g in weight, a variety of your choice)

235g caster sugar

80ml water

juice of half a lemon

drop of orange blossom water (optional)

For the buckwheat sliha
200g cooked buckwheat

2 tbsp fennel seeds

125g pine nuts

125g walnuts

55g demerara sugar

30g pomegranate seeds

½ tsp cinnamon

½ tsp salt

For the cheesecake filling
1300g full-fat soft cheese

440g caster sugar

Zest of 1 orange

40g plain flour

120ml double cream

5 eggs plus 3 eggs yolks

1 tbsp orange blossom water

For the cheesecake crust
150g digestive biscuits

75g unsalted butter - melted

¼ tsp baharat spice blend or cinnamon

When I started my research of Syrian sweets the combination of sweet cheese, pastry, nuts and orange blossom was very prevalent. My recipe is a combination of these elements.

Grease and line a 26cm Springform cake tin

For the candied pumpkin
Preheat oven to 170°C – cut the pumpkin/squash in half and remove seeds.
Roast pumpkin/squash cut-side down for approximately 30 mins until flesh is tender and scoopable.

Meanwhile, prepare sugar syrup. Combine water, sugar and lemon juice in a pan and bring to the boil. Reduce to a simmer and cook until thick and syrupy (around 10 mins); add orange blossom if using. Scoop flesh from pumpkin/squash and add to syrup.

For the buckwheat sliha
Set oven to 180°C. Combine buckwheat groats, fennel seeds and 400ml water in a pan. Bring to the boil; cover, reduce to a simmer and cook until tender (about 10 mins).

Drain and dry buckwheat on a flat tray. Roast nuts until lightly golden; cool and chop roughly. Once buckwheat is dry, roast on baking tray until crispy. Combine the nuts, pomegranate seeds, sugar, cinnamon, salt, cooled buckwheat and fennel-seed mix.

Cheesecake
For the crust: Blitz the biscuits in a food processor until fine crumbs and add the cinnamon. Add the melted butter until combined. Press the biscuit mix into the base of the tin.

Cook base at 180°C for 10-12 mins and cool in the fridge. Once cool, rub butter around the sides of the tin, sprinkling with caster sugar. Case the whole tin in foil before baking whole cheesecake.

For the filling
Mix cream cheese with sugar using a mixer with paddle attachment on slowest setting until very smooth.

In a separate bowl, use whisk attachment to whip eggs until light and fluffy. Add double cream to egg mix and whisk until incorporated; then fold the flour using a spatula until combined. Fold egg mix into cheese mix. Add orange blossom water.

Bake at 180°C for 15 mins, then open the door and let the oven cool to 100°C and bake at 100°C for another 35 mins.

Let cheesecake cool for 90 mins in oven before refrigerating.

CAKES

Photography by @CharlotteHuCo
Styling by @lily_vanilli_cake

SFOUF (TURMERIC CAKE) WITH CHOCOLATE RASPBERRY LABNEH

Donated by Sharon Salloum of Almond Bar
@almondbar

"We are thrilled to take part in an incredible movement that encompasses a major part of Syrian culture – sharing food, giving, learning from one another. Our parents are both one of nine children and we have sixteen aunties and uncles, many of whom are still in Syria. We are fortunate that they have mostly not been affected physically by the conflict, but we know many who have been and our family could be much worse off. If you can help someone in some small way then why wouldn't you?"

Serves 8

For the cake

2 cups (440 g) fine semolina

160 g plain flour

¾ tsp turmeric powder

1 tsp baking powder

250g butter, melted and cooled for 15 mins

1 ¾ cups (385g) sugar

1 ½ cups (375ml) milk

1 ½ tbsp hulled tahini

½ cup (70g) raw slivered almonds

For the labneh

190g cooking milk chocolate, roughly chopped

400ml labneh

100ml thickened cream, whipped

25 whole raspberries

I have been eating Syrian and Middle Eastern food since I could be given solids. It's in my DNA and I can't imagine life without it. I've spent many hours in local Middle Eastern sweets stores wondering about this mysterious cake. It is a much-loved "tea-style" cake and I have always adored the way it looks. The subtle use of turmeric makes it stand out not just in terms of flavour, but visually as well. It is a soft, delicate cake because of the semolina and its buttery texture leaves you wanting more.

Preheat the oven to 180°C (fan).

Place the semolina, flour, turmeric, and baking powder into a large bowl and stir to combine.

In a separate bowl, combine the cooled butter, sugar, milk and 60ml water. Whisk until at least half of the sugar has dissolved. Pour into the dry ingredients and stir to make a thick batter.

Grease a deep 23cm round cake tin by rubbing the tahini all over the base and sides with the tips of your fingers.

Pour the cake batter into the tin and sprinkle with slivered almonds. Bake for 40-45 mins or until the cake is browned on top.

Whilst waiting for the cake to cook, make the chocolate raspberry labneh. Start by melting the chocolate in a double boiler. You can do this by placing some water in a medium saucepan, putting it on a medium heat and sitting a stainless steel bowl on the top of the saucepan, allowing the steam to warm the bowl. Place the cooking chocolate in the stainless steel bowl and allow it to melt, using a wooden spoon or spatula to scrape down the sides and cook the chocolate evenly.

In a separate bowl, place the labneh, whipped cream and raspberry together. Once the chocolate has melted and is completely smooth, scrape it into the bowl of labneh and quickly work it through the ingredients so as to avoid any large solid chunks of chocolate forming (small ones are okay). You can also break up the raspberries a little while doing this. Set aside in the fridge until required.

Remove the cake from the oven and cool in the tin for about 10 mins, then turn the cake out onto a wire rack to cool completely. Serve with the chocolate raspberry labneh, coffee or tea. Store in an airtight container for up to a week.

Photography by @KatieWilsonFoto
Styling by @lily_vanilli_cake

BLOOD ORANGE & ALMOND CAKE GF, DF, V

Donated by Deliciously Ella
@deliciouslyella

"It's just an incredible project. I love how it brings people together, uniting them through a love of food and creating awareness of such an important issue."

Serves 12

For the cake

300g ground almonds

240g buckwheat flour

1 tbsp of bicarbonate of soda

Pinch of sea salt

The water from x1 400g can of chickpeas, not the chickpeas themselves

440ml maple syrup

100ml almond milk

To serve:

2 blood oranges, plus the zest of 1

a handful of pistachios, roughly chopped

200g natural yoghurt (I use coconut)

2 tbsp of maple syrup

This blood orange and almond cake is so delicious and full of rich flavours. It's a vegan sponge, so we use chickpea water to make it light and fluffy – I know it sounds strange but it really does work, while the maple adds a lovely sweetness. It's baked with a layer of blood orange slices and topped with a smooth layer of coconut yoghurt, orange zest and crunchy pieces of pistachio.

Preheat oven to 180°C fan.

In a large bowl mix together ground almonds, buckwheat flour, bicarb and salt, giving it all a really good stir to remove any lumps. When the mixture is well combined add in the maple syrup, almond milk and chickpea water – mixing it all until it comes together to form a batter.

Cut the blood orange into thin slices, and then in halves. Place the slices at the bottom of a lined cake tin, overlapping, around the edge of the tin. Once your slices are in place, pour the cake mixture over the top and cook in the oven for 45-50 mins until cooked through. Once cooked, remove from the oven and leave to cool at room temperature.

Next make your icing by placing the coconut yoghurt in a large bowl and mix until it becomes really thick, around 5-8 mins using an electric mixer. Once its thickened, add in your maple syrup and continue mixing for another minute. If you don't have an electric mixer you can do it by hand – just make sure you mix it long enough to get a good amount of air and thickness into it, about 15-20 mins.

Once the cake has cooled, turn it out onto a large dish and spoon on your coconut icing into the middle. Sprinkle with a handful of chopped pistachios and the zest of 1 blood orange.

Photography by @hollyfarrierphotography
Portrait by @Sophia_Spring_Photography

HONEY LOAF W/ ROSE DUKKAH AND TAHINI CREAM

Donated by Alex Hely-Hutchinson of 26 Grains
@26grains

"I've admired this campaign and what it has done for putting the refugee crisis at the forefront of conversation. We eat and cook everyday and food can be a way of bringing communities together. #BakeForSyria is a great example of how food can continue to make a positive difference."

For the loaf
175g spelt flour
125g ground almonds
2 tsp baking powder
1 pinch flaked sea salt
225g unsalted butter, softened
250g demerara sugar
140ml honey
zest of 1 orange
4 large eggs

For the dukkah
40g almonds
40g black sesame seeds
2 tsp cumin seeds
2 tsp coriander seeds
1 tsp fennel seeds
1 tsp salt
ground black pepper

For the syrup
4 tbsp honey
4 tbsp dukkah
1 tsp rose water
juice of 1 orange

For the tahini cream
125ml Greek yoghurt
125ml double cream
2 tsp honey
3 tsp tahini
1/2 tsp vanilla

Middle Eastern baking always reminds me of sweet nuts and compact textures and I wanted to celebrate this in our recipe. The ground almonds in the cake gives it that tight rich texture, and the nuts and spices on top remind me of those little clusters you find in baklava. This recipe is simple, sweet, spiced and has a lovely moist texture contrasted by the bite of the dukkah. You can make it as a cake or how we like it, in a loaf tin.

Preheat oven to 170°C

Mix all the dry ingredients together; spelt flour, almonds, baking powder, salt.

Beat butter, sugar, honey and orange together until creamy. Add the eggs.

Pour dry mix in and fold through.

Grease and line X1 loaf tin. Spoon in mixture and bake for approx. 45-50 mins, until springy.

Make the dukkah by lightly crushing all the ingredients. Roast at 180°C until lightly golden and fragrant.

Gently whisk the tahini cream ingredients together until it begins to thicken. Be careful not to over whisk.

Once the cake has been removed from the oven, heat the syrup ingredients on medium-high heat, add the dukkah mix and simmer until slightly reduced. Prick the cake and drizzle over the syrup. Leave to cool in tin.

Serve cake with tahini cream.

Photography by @KatieWilsonFoto
Styling by @lily_vanilli_cake

ALMOND, CARDAMOM AND DATE CAKE GF

Donated by Jordan Bourke
@jordanbourke

"For me, cooking and baking in particular has always been about family, coming together and being thankful. Now, cooking with my young son I feel even more keenly the importance of raising money to support the children of Syria."

Serves 10

200g raw almonds

100g desiccated coconut

100g pitted medjool dates

3 eggs, beaten

150g light brown sugar or coconut palm sugar

150ml sunflower oil

60ml coconut or rice milk

8 cardamom pods, shells removed and ground to a powder

finely grated zest of 1 unwaxed lemon

1 tsp baking powder

¼ tsp sea salt

1 tsp vanilla extract

1 tsp of rose water

To serve

4 tbsp coconut flakes, lightly roasted

2 tbsp dried rose petals

250g Greek yoghurt

This cake came together one winter evening when my wife had a hankering for something sweet. I made the most of some leftover ingredients I had, including coconut milk, medjool dates and rose water. The result is an incredibly moist and fragrant wheat-free cake which is not cloyingly sweet, making it perfect for any time of day. In fact, my wife and I sometimes have a slice for breakfast. A dollop of Greek yoghurt or crème fraiche cuts through the richness of the cake perfectly.

Line a 20cm springform cake tin with parchment paper. Preheat the oven to 170°C or 150°C fan.

Place the almonds and desiccated coconut in a food processor and blitz until the almonds are very finely chopped, but not a paste, remove to a large mixing bowl and set aside. Add the dates and eggs into the processor and blitz until the dates are finely chopped and mixed into the eggs. Add into the bowl with the almonds and the rest of the cake ingredients and mix thoroughly until well combined.

Pour into the cake tin and level out, bake in the centre of the oven for 40-45 mins or until a skewer comes out mostly clean. If the top is browning to quickly, cover with foil. Remove and leave to cool for 10 mins, then remove from the tin to a cooling rack.

When ready to serve, pile the coconut chips and rose petals onto the centre of the cake. This cake is particularly nice served a little warm with the cool yoghurt on the side.

LIME CURD AND HARISSA DRIZZLE CAKE GF

Donated by Pip McCormac
@pipmccormac

"Wandering around the first #BakeForSyria sale on London's Columbia Road, I was struck by how proud I was of the food community. My friends and colleagues had put Instagram down and were doing something good for those who needed it. Of course I wanted to be involved, I felt inspired to be a better human. It's amazing what a piece of cake can make you feel."

Serves 6-8

For the lime curd
2 yolks
zest and juice of 3 limes
100g sugar
50g butter

For the cake
300g ground almonds
3 eggs
100g sugar
2 tsp baking powder
½ tsp red harissa

For the syrup
juice and zest of 1 lime
juice of ½ a lemon
1 tbsp honey

For this recipe, I have made a cake using harissa (a spicy paste used in savoury dishes) paired with lime and almonds and sugar – and it works! You don't need too much harissa – just enough to be left with a gentle warmth, a hint of a punch that really lifts this elegant cake into the world of the sublime. I like the slow, meditative stirring of the three sections, the excitement of unexpected flavours and the joy of a new cake to eat.

Tip: You could make this cake entirely gluten free by using gluten-free baking powder, or dairy-free by substituting the butter for olive oil.

Preheat the oven to 180°C/gas mark 4. Grease and line a deep 20cm springform round tin.

First make the curd. Put all the ingredients into a small pan and place over a low heat, stirring as it gently comes to a boil. Simmer for 15 mins, stirring occasionally, until it begins to thicken and coat the spoon a little. Remove from the heat and set aside.

Put all of the ingredients for the cake into the bowl of an electric mixer and beat until well combined, before pouring in the curd and beating well. Tip this into the prepared tin and smooth the surface the knife. Bake in the oven for 30 mins, until you can put a point of a knife into the middle and it comes out clean. Allow to cool for a few minutes in the tin before turning it out onto a wire rack.

Put the ingredients for the syrup into a small pan over a medium heat and simmer for 5 mins or so until reduced and nicely thick.

Once the cake is completely cold, put it on a plate with high edges and use a sharp knife to puncture holes in the top. Pour the syrup over the cake and allow it to sink in for a couple of mins before serving.

Photography by @CharlotteHuCo
Styling by @lily_vanilli_cake

CLEMENTINE, PISTACHIO AND POMEGRANATE CAKE
GF, DF

Donated by Amelia Freer
@AmeliaFreer

"The kitchen is the heart of the home and therefore transcends many of the barriers that separate us, from language to culture. Bringing communities and cooks together to celebrate that which unites us while raising much-needed funds for those in need, #BakeForSyria is an amazing initiative. I feel very privileged to play a small part in it.."

For the cake

4-5 whole clementines depending on size, (roughly 360g) skin on

5 eggs

130g honey

1 tbsp orange blossom water

50g tahini

275 ground almonds

1 ½ tsp baking powder

60g pistachios, ideally soaked in water or a couple of hours

125g pomegranate seeds or from half a pomegranate

This recipe is an adaptation of the lemon cake I used to make and I love the alchemy of it. You combine all sorts of ingredients you wouldn't necessarily expect to find in a cake – as well as leaving out many you would – and still manage to end up with the most divine, indulgent bake at the end of the cooking time. It is flour-free and has whole blended clementines in the mixture which makes it pretty runny, but I promise that once baked it miraculously transforms into a delicious, delicately flavoured and moist cake with all the evocative scents of the Middle East. Bejewelled with green pistachios and juicy pomegranate seeds, it's a joy to make and to eat. It's also gluten and dairy free.

Put the clementines in a saucepan and cover with plenty of water. Bring to the boil, then turn down the heat and simmer gently for 45 mins for small clementines or 1 hour for larger ones. This works best if they are submerged in the water, so place a smaller saucepan on top to weigh them down. Keep an eye on the water level, adding more if necessary. Drain and leave until cool enough to handle.

Preheat the oven to 160fan/180.

Grease and line a 23cm (9"), loose bottom cake tin.

Cut the clementines in half, remove any pips and blend, with skins on, in a food processor until smooth.

Add the eggs, honey, orange water and tahini blending to combine then add the ground almonds and baking powder and blend just until mixed – don't over mix this stage.

Roughly chop the pistachios (save a few for decoration) and add them to the mix along with 2/3 of the pomegranate seeds, stirring gently through.

Pour the batter into the cake tin, smoothing the top and bake for 50 mins or until a skewer comes out clean. You may need to cover the top with baking paper halfway through to stop the top over-browning.

Allow to cool in the tin and turn out once cooled. Decorate with chopped pistachios and pomegranate seeds.

Photography by @CharlotteHuCo
Portrait by @KatieWilsonFoto
Styling by @lily_vanilli_cake

PISTACHIO, POLENTA AND YOGHURT CAKE GF

Donated by Anna Jones
@we_are_food

"I have boundless admiration for the amazing team who put Cook and #BakeForSyria together, from the chefs and bakers to the brilliant supporters, it's just wonderful to see food doing good for a much needed cause."

Serves 8

For the cake

125g butter, at room temperature

125g Greek yoghurt

250g light brown sugar or coconut sugar

250g pistachio nuts

200g polenta

1 tsp baking powder

Grated zest and juice of 1 unwaxed orange

3 organic or free-range eggs

2 tbsp of orange blossom water

For the orange blossom yoghurt icing

100g thick Greek yoghurt or cream cheese

4 tbsp golden icing sugar or set honey

1-2 tsp orange blossom water

1 handful of pistachio nuts, crushed

This pistachio, polenta and yoghurt cake is everything I want in a cake - a beautiful crumb and fragrant flavour. A cake that does good.

Preheat your oven to 200°C. Grease and line the base of a 20cm springform cake tin.

Put the butter, yoghurt and sugar into a bowl and cream together until light and fluffy.

Now blitz the pistachios to dust in a food processor – don't blitz them too much, though, or they will turn to butter.

Add the blitzed pistachios, polenta, baking powder and orange zest and juice to the butter mixture and mix well. Then crack in the eggs, one by one, and mix in.

Pour into a 20cm springform cake tin and bake for 45–50 mins, until a skewer comes out clean. Remove from the oven and leave to cool in the tin. Make a few holes in the warm cake with a skewer, then gently pour the orange blossom water slowly over the cake, allowing it time to seep in.

Leave the cake in the tin until cool enough to transfer to a cooling rack.

For the icing
Mix the yoghurt, icing sugar or honey and orange blossom water until smooth.

Spread over the cooled cake and top with the pistachios.

Photography by John Dale
Portrait by @KatieWilsonFoto

PEAR AND PISTACHIO CAKE

Donated by David McGuinness of Bourke Street Bakery
@bourkestreetbakery

"A few years back, Bourke Street Bakery helped set up a wholesale bakery called The Bread and Butter Project. This bakery is a social enterprise that trains refugees and asylum seekers in the art of making artisan bread. We are fortunate to have been able to help many people from different countries, including Syria. Being included in this book is an honour and offers us another way to help."

For the cake

240g milk

5g bicarbonate of soda

300g plain flour

100g ground pistachio

10g baking powder

240g brown sugar

170g butter

8g nutmeg

¼ tsp whole vanilla bean

1 egg

50gms whole pistachios

20 segments Poached pear

20ml honey

This recipe has been adapted from a cake I know of by the name of "Middle Eastern Love Cake", which I think is the best ever name for a cake. It is a simple and flavoursome cake. I love the way the batter is split before baking to form a crust and a cake from the same mix. It can be adapted in various ways. The pears can be swapped for quince or stone fruits, or the fruit can be completely omitted. The pistachios could be swapped with almonds or walnuts. I bake it at Bourke Street during Quince season as a special a couple of times a week.

Preheat oven to 180°C

Remove butter from fridge 20 mins before starting the recipe.

Mix bicarbonate of soda with milk and set aside. Dice the butter into 2cm cubes. Place flour, baking powder, brown sugar and butter in a stainless steel bowl. Rub together with your fingertips until it resembles fine bread crumbs. Divide mixture into two even portions. Gently press one portion into a 28cmx3.5cm deep loose bottom fluted tart mould. Place in the oven to bake for 10 mins.

Add nutmeg to the second portion. Whilst the base is baking, whisk the eggs lightly and stir in the milk-bicarb mix. Slowly add the liquid to the flour mix, whisking to form a batter, then fold through the ground pistachios.

Remove the base from the oven, pour the batter over it. Place pears in a circular pattern on top of the batter and sprinkle with the whole pistachios.

Bake for 30-40 mins at 165-170°C, turning halfway through baking if necessary. Test with skewer. The cake is ready when skewer comes out clean.

Warm honey in a pan whilst cake is baking.

Remove cake from oven and brush with warmed honey.

Remove from the mould, cut and serve warm, or allow to cool and serve at room temperature.

Perfect served with yoghurt.

PISTACHIO CAKE WITH ORANGE BLOSSOM MASCARPONE ICING AND PISTACHIO BRITTLE

Donated by Alexandra Dudley
@alexandradudley

"The #BakeForSyria and #CookForSyria campaigns are thoughtful responses to the crisis, because they combine charity and celebration. It's brilliant to raise money but I believe equally important to celebrate Syria's rich culture. The initiative increases awareness of the conflict while encouraging appreciation of a people without whom we would have a blander palate. I have supported it from day one."

For the cake
2 large Navel oranges
250g whole almonds
70g pistachios, roughly chopped
5 eggs
250g caster sugar
1 tsp baking powder

For the pistachio brittle
70g unsalted butter
120g caster sugar
4 tbsp honey
Pinch of vanilla powder
150g pistachios, roughly chopped

For the icing
250g mascarpone cheese (at room temperature)
100g icing sugar sieved
½ tsp orange blossom water

I remember the first time I made orange cake. It was with a good friend of mine who is a fabulous cook. She served it the Italian way dusted with icing sugar and it was delicious. For a Syrian twist, I have added orange blossom and pistachio brittle which gives the cake a celebratory flair.

Grease and line the base of an 8 inch springform cake tin. Preheat your oven to 180°C fan.

Bake almonds on a tray for 12-15 mins or until fragrant. Shake halfway and ensure they don't burn. Remove and cool. Switch oven off.

In a large saucepan place your whole oranges and cover with cold water. Bring to the boil before partially covering with a lid and reducing the temperature to a simmer. Simmer for two hours topping up the water as necessary. Drain and cool.

Once cool, preheat your oven to 180°C fan again.

Blitz almonds in a food processor until you have a flour like texture. Transfer to a bowl.

Next, quarter your oranges and remove pips before placing them in the food processor and pulsing to a purée.

In a large bowl, electric whisk your eggs and sugar until thick and pale in colour.

Stir in your almonds, baking powder and oranges until well combined.
Then lightly fold in chopped pistachios. Pour mix into the prepared tin and bake for about 60 mins or until done.

Allow the to cool in the tin for 40 mins before removing the sides and cooling completely.

For the brittle: place butter, sugar and honey in a saucepan over medium heat and stir until butter and sugar have melted. Continue to stir whilst it cooks and caramelizes, about 8 mins.

Once the mix is ready, mix pistachios in quickly then tip onto your sheet and spread out with an oiled spatula. Firm up in the fridge before snapping into shards.

For the icing: place mascarpone, orange blossom water and sieved icing sugar in a large bowl and beat together.

Ice and decorate your cake.

Photography by Holly Wulf Peterson
Styling by @alexandradudley

CLEMENTINE AND POMEGRANATE CAKE GF, DF

Donated by Eric Lanlard of Cake Boy
@eric_lanlard

"Sadness is a major reason for taking part in this amazing campaign. I still find it difficult to understand how in today's world people can be so destructive. Such devastation in a beautiful country full of history is a tragedy. The pictures and reports of the terrible conditions faced by Syrian refugees are heartbreaking, especially considering how many children are involved. It was a no-brainer when I was asked to take part."

Serves 12

For the cake

4 clementines or satsumas, unpeeled

1 cinnamon stick

Oil, for greasing

6 large eggs

225g (8oz) light muscovado sugar

1 tsp gluten-free baking powder

300g (10 ½ oz) ground almonds

For the syrup

1 pomegranate, halved

25g (1oz) light muscovado sugar

1 tsp orange blossom extract

1 tsp vanilla bean paste

To decorate

3 tbsp apricot glaze

icing sugar, for dusting

My Grandparents lived in Syria for a few years. Once back in France, their travels inspired their cooking. My grandmother's spice rack was a piece of culinary genius. She was like a conductor orchestrating all her spices to create special dishes and bakes. That was my first introduction to Middle Eastern cooking. Now all my favourite ingredients hail from there and this is one of my favourite recipes. It's a feast for the eyes, with beautiful jewel-like pomegranate seeds that look like rubies. It happens also to be gluten and dairy free.

This recipe originally appeared in Eric Lanlard's Afternoon Tea published by Mitchell Beazley

Put the clementines and cinnamon into a medium saucepan, cover with cold water and bring to the boil.

Reduce the heat, cover with a lid and simmer for 1–1½ hours, then drain the fruit and remove the cinnamon stick. Leave to cool for 30 mins.

Halve the cooked fruit and discard the pips. Put the fruit, with peel, into a blender or food processor and blend to a purée. Set aside.

Preheat the oven to 180°C. Grease a 23cm (9in) diameter, 9cm (3 ½ in) deep cake tin and line with baking paper.

Whisk the eggs and sugar in a heatproof bowl over a saucepan of barely simmering water for about 5 mins until pale and mousse-like.

Take the bowl off the heat and add the baking powder, ground almonds and fruit puree. Fold in gently but thoroughly.

Spoon the mixture into the tin and bake for 20 mins. Reduce the temperature to 160°C and bake for 30 mins, or until a skewer inserted into the centre comes out clean, then allow to cool completely.

To make the syrup, squeeze the pomegranate halves to extract the juice, reserving the seeds, then pour the juice into a small saucepan. Add sugar and bring to the boil, then simmer for 2 mins. Leave to cool slightly (the liquid should still be warm), then stir in the orange blossom extract and vanilla paste. Using a pastry brush, 'soak' the cake with the warm pomegranate syrup and leave in the tin until completely cold.

Transfer the cake to a plate, brush the apricot glaze all over the cake, including the sides, scatter the reserved pomegranate seeds over the top and dust with icing sugar.

CAKES

Photography by @KatieWilsonFoto
Styling by @lily_vanilli_cake

DRIED APRICOT & SEMOLINA SYRUP CAKE WITH PISTACHIOS

Donated by Maggie Beer
@Maggie_Beer

"I was thrilled to be asked to donate a recipe for this important book and support those who have been so affected by the war in Syria. No child should have to live in fear or feel insecure – so here's hoping that through the wonderful work of Unicef UK and this special cookbook, we can incite change and give these children a better life."

Serves 12-14

300g unsalted butter, softened
150g (¾ cup) caster sugar
6 free range eggs
225g (1 cup) natural Greek yoghurt
250g (2 ½ cups) almond meal
200g (1 cup) fine semolina
1 tspn baking powder

375ml (1 ½ cups) water
330ml (1 ¼ cups) verjuice
350g dried apricots
250ml (1 cup) honey
200g (1 cup) caster sugar

50g unsalted pistachios, roughly chopped

These are all the flavours I love so much; they are flavours of the Middle East but also of the Mediterranean climate I live in. We grow and dry our own apricots; we make our verjuice from unripe grapes; we have our own honey and though we don't have our own pistachios, they grow wonderfully in our climate. I don't have to tell you that there is nothing quite like the smell of a freshly baked cake – and you can enjoy this cake knowing that you've helped raise awareness and much needed money for UNICEF UK's Children of Syria Appeal.

Preheat a fan oven to 160°C.

Grease a 25cm springform cake tin, set aside.

For the cake
Cream butter and sugar on a high speed until light and creamy.

Reduce the speed and add the eggs, one at a time. Once combined, add the yoghurt and continue to mix on a medium speed for 2 mins or until well combined. At this stage the mixture will appear split, which is normal.

With the mixer on a low speed, add the almond meal, semolina and baking powder. Mix until well combined and of smooth consistency.

Pour batter into the greased tin and place into the oven. Rotate the cake after 40 mins and if the top is becoming too dark, lightly cover with foil. Bake for a further 15 mins or until a skewer inserted in the centre comes out clean. Place cake, still in its tin, onto a wire rack to cool.

Meanwhile, pour the water and verjuice into a large saucepan over a high heat. Bring to a simmer, then add the apricots and cook for 3 mins before scooping out and placing them onto a plate. Add the honey and sugar to the saucepan, bring to the boil, then lower and simmer for 10 mins.

Return apricots to the syrup and remove from the heat. Allow to steep for 5 mins, then strain, setting aside both the apricots and the syrup.

Whilst still in its tin, slowly pour the warm syrup over the cake, allowing it to really soak in. Remove cake from tin and place onto your plate. Evenly distribute the apricots on top, sprinkle with pistachios and serve.

Photography by Olivia Barton
Portrait by Eliza Harley

PERSIAN FRUIT CAKE

Donated by Martha Collison
@marthacollison

"I am an ambassador for the charity Tearfund and recently visited Lebanon to see the work being done to help refugee families who have fled Syria due to the awful conflict. I spent time in the camps, and with families in their homes. I was blown away by hospitality lavished on us by people who have been left with nothing, and shocked at the conditions children were growing up in. #BakeForSyria is making a positive difference, bringing hope in a place of such trauma."

SERVES 16

For the cake

200g prunes, cut into small pieces

150g dried figs, cut into small pieces

200g dried apricots, cut into small pieces

150g chopped dates

50g piece candied orange peel, cut into small pieces

grated zest of 1 unwaxed lemon

1 tsp rose water

200g butter, plus extra for greasing

200g soft light brown sugar

150g runny honey

3 large eggs, beaten

200g self-raising flour

100g ground almonds

Rose syrup

150g caster sugar

2 tsp rose water

Pistachio marzipan

200g pistachio nuts

100g icing sugar, plus extra for dusting

100g caster sugar

1 large egg white

dried rose petals and chopped pistachios, to decorate

You will also need a 20cm loose-bottomed

Fruit cake seems to have earned itself a bad reputation among young people; I am one of those who can't get excited about over-rich Christmas cake where the only enjoyable bit is picking the icing on the top. But even if you are a fruit-cake hater like me, I ask you to look at this cake with fresh eyes. The Middle East produces an array of incredible dried fruits, and this cake is an ode to them; a celebration of beautiful fruits and nuts, all gently melded together with a sticky rose syrup.

Grease the cake tin and line the base and sides with a double layer of baking parchment. This will stop the sides of the cake browning too much.

Place the dried fruits in a large saucepan. Add the lemon zest, rose water, butter, sugar and honey, and place the pan over a medium heat. Heat gently, stirring all the time, until the butter melts, then simmer for about 10 mins. Remove from the heat and leave to cool for about 30 mins. Pre-heat the oven to 160°C/140°C fan/gas 2 while you are waiting for the mixture to cool.

Beat the eggs into the cooled fruit mix, then stir in the flour and ground almonds until well combined. Pour the cake mixture into the lined tin and bake for 1 3/4–2 hours or until a skewer inserted into the centre comes out clean and the top of the cake feels dry.

While the cake is baking, make the rose syrup. Combine the sugar and rose water with 75ml of water in a small saucepan and simmer over a medium heat until all the sugar grains have dissolved. Cook the syrup for a further 30 seconds, then remove from the heat and allow to cool completely.

When the cake has been cooling for 5 mins, pierce small holes over the surface of the fruit cake and feed it with the rose syrup, using a pastry brush to apply the syrup and letting the cake absorb as much syrup as it can. This will make the fruit cake very moist. Leave the cake to cool completely in the tin.

To make the pistachio marzipan, blitz the pistachio nuts, icing sugar and caster sugar together in a food processor until they form a really fine powder. Add the egg white and blend again until the mixture clumps together. Wrap the marzipan in cling film until ready to use.

Lightly dust a worktop with icing sugar and roll out the marzipan (or roll it between 2 pieces of cling film) to make a disc the same size as the top of the cake. Press the marzipan on to the top of the cake, then sprinkle on the rose petals and chopped pistachio nuts.

Photography by @laurajayneedwards

2. PASTRY & DOUGHS

—

BIRD'S NEST

Donated by Imad Alarnab
@imadssyriankitchen

"As a Syrian living in London it is my duty to represent the wonderful cuisine of my home country and to do as much as possible to help others who have lost their homes and loved ones. I'm honoured to be a part of this project because of the amazing aims it has and the awareness it has created. I have made many new friendships though this initiative and hope we can continue to do more good work together."

Makes approx 20

For the bird's nest:

300g of kanafeh.

approx. 1 and 1/2 cups of melted butter

For the fillings:

two cups of pistachio

two cups of water

two cups of sugar

two big spoons of lemon juice

Bird's Nest is a kind of sweet that originated in Syrian cuisine and then spread to all the countries of the Arab world. This Bird's Nest recipe is easy to prepare and has an extremely delicious and special taste. It is also beautiful thanks to the fine kanafeh.

For Qater (Syrup)

Combine sugar and water in a pan and swirl a little to combine.
Place it over a medium heat to melt sugar and boil for a minute, then add the lemon, stir and heat for another minute.

Cover the kanafeh with a damp cloth while you work so that it does not dry out.

Take a piece of kanafeh and wrap it around your thumb or two fingers to form a nest shape, and transfer it to a lined baking sheet.

Repeat the process for the rest of the kanafeh.

Press pistachios into the centre of your kanafeh nests.

Cover the oven tray with baking paper, then another oven tray. Place a 1kg weight over it, then leave at room temperature for 2 hours, remove the paper and leave it for another hour.

Pour the butter in your oven tray and put the tray in an oven preheated to 22°C for 20-25 mins, turning from time to time.

Drizzle with the warm syrup and serve

Photography by @KatieWilsonFoto
Styling by @lily_vanilli_cake

ATAYEF (PANCAKES) WITH RICOTTA, DATES & CARDAMOM HONEY

Donated by John Whaite
@john_whaite

"This dish was inspired by the communality of food. Pancakes, for example, cross borders and religions – from Easter to Eid."

Serves 8-10

For the batter
55g plain flour
a pinch of salt
2 large eggs
115ml whole milk
sunflower oil, for frying

For the filling
175g stoned dates
175g ricotta
zest of 1 small orange

For the frying and honey
750ml sunflower oil
200g runny honey
3 cardamom pods, bruised
50g pistachio nuts, roughly crushed

This whole campaign is about recognising and embracing humanity, as well as the need for us all to protect that beautiful thing that we take for granted: life. And food is the ultimate giver of life.

To make the batter, mix together the flour and salt in a small bowl. Make a well in the centre, crack in the eggs and add a good splash of the milk. Whisk the ingredients together to form a smooth, thick batter, then slowly add the rest of the milk, whisking.

Before you cook the pancakes, dampen a clean tea towel to cover the pancakes – it's important that they don't dry out.

In a good non-stick frying pan, heat a small amount of oil over a high heat. Once the pan starts to haze, reduce the heat to medium/low. Add a tablespoon of batter, spread to a disk of about four inches in diameter, and allow to cook just until the upper surface becomes dull and satiny, and pinprick bubbles appear – about 30 seconds. Using a pallete knife or fish slice, lift the pancake on to a large plate – cooked side down – and cover with the tea towel. Repeat until you have used all the batter – you may need to add a little more oil to the pan every five or six pancakes.

To make the filling, chop the dates, as finely as is humanly possible – though I prefer the mechanical help of a food processor. Beat together with the ricotta and zest to form a thick paste.

Take a pancake in your hand, cooked side down in the palm, and place a heaped teaspoon of the filling onto the centre. Fold the pancake in half, encasing the filling, and pinch the meeting edges together firmly – rather like a pixie-sized pasty.

To fry, heat the oil in a heavy-based saucepan or wok, until it reaches 180C/355F, or until a cube of bread sizzles frantically when dropped in. Add the atayefs, four at a time, and fry until a medium/dark golden brown. Remove from the oil and drain on a piece of kitchen towel.

For the honey drizzle, heat the honey and cardamom in a small saucepan until very runny.

To serve, dip or drench the atayef in the honey, then top with pistachio pieces.

DOUGHNUTS WITH SAFFRON CUSTARD AND CANDIED PISTACHIOS

Donated by Michael James of Tivoli Road
@tivolirdbakery

"To help the people of Syria by doing something that we love and to share what we do at the bakery is a no brainer. It's so exciting to see bakers and chefs unite and give up their time to help people who need it most. As with #CookForSyria, I hope readers can gain more knowledge of the kinds of ingredients used in and around Syria and shine a light on its beautiful and rich culture."

For the doughnuts
190g bakers flour

25g caster sugar

2g salt

Zest of one lemon

8g fresh yeast

40g water

10g lemon oil

2 medium eggs, at room temperature

45g butter, diced and soft

1 litre vegetable oil, such as rice bran or cottonseed oil, for deep-frying

Cinnamon sugar
125g caster sugar

½ tsp ground cinnamon

Centuries ago the Cornish would trade tin and copper for items from the Middle East such as saffron, and saffron cake and buns are still sold all around Cornwall today. One of my introductions to baking was helping my Gran make saffron cake as a child growing up in Cornwall. For this recipe, I could not think of a better combination than doughnuts and the saffron from my childhood roots in aid of such a worthy cause. The fragrant and luxurious saffron cream balances the crunchy sweetness of the pistachios perfectly in this well-fermented, yeasty doughnut.

For the doughnuts
Mix the flour, sugar, salt and lemon zest in a bowl, and set aside. Combine the yeast, half the water, lemon oil and eggs in the bowl of an electric mixer fitted with the dough hook. Add the flour mixture and mix on medium speed for 10 mins, adding more water as needed to make a smooth dough.

Add the softened butter slowly while continuing to mix. Mix for 5 mins, until the butter is fully incorporated. The dough should come away from the bowl and form a ball that is smooth, shiny and slightly sticky. Use the windowpane test to check the dough – take a small ball of dough and gently stretch it between your hands. You should be able to stretch it very thin without it breaking. When it's ready, leave the dough to rest in the bowl, covered with a damp tea towel, for 1 hour.

After an hour, knock back the dough and fold it by lifting one side up and over the other. Do this five or six times. Transfer the dough to a lightly oiled container, then cover again and refrigerate overnight.

Line two trays with baking paper, and spray lightly with oil. Turn the dough out onto a lightly floured bench and cut into 10 equal pieces. Gently flatten each one and bring the edges together in the middle to form a rough ball, and then flip so the seam is at the bottom. Cup your hand over the dough and roll it on the bench to form a tight round ball. Place the doughnuts on the tray and cover again with the damp tea towel, leaving them to rest for 15-20 mins.

Take each doughnut and knock it flat, then fold the edges into the middle and turn it over so the seam is at the bottom. Using firm pressure, roll it in your hand on the bench again. Putting pressure on the doughnuts strengthens the dough for the eventual rise. Lightly cover with plastic wrap and leave to rise for 2-3 hours, or until risen by half. Test the doughnuts by gently pressing the surface. If this leaves a dent, they're ready to fry, but if the dough springs back it still needs more time.

Photography by @bonniesavage
Styling by @charlieduffy__

DOUGHNUTS WITH SAFFRON CUSTARD AND CANDIED PISTACHIOS

Donated by Michael James of Tivoli Road
@tivolirdbakery

"To help the people of Syria by doing something that we love and to share what we do at the bakery is a no brainer. It's so exciting to see bakers and chefs unite and give up their time to help people who need it most. As with #CookForSyria, I hope readers can gain more knowledge of the kinds of ingredients used in and around Syria and shine a light on its beautiful and rich culture."

For the custard
300g full cream milk
Pinch of saffron
3 egg yolks
30g caster sugar
40g plain flour

For the pistachios
150g green pistachios
90g water
45g sugar

Heat the oil for deep-frying to 180°C in a large, heavy based saucepan or deep fryer. Fry the doughnuts a few at a time, for about a minute on each side, until golden. Use a slotted spoon to turn them and remove them from the oil, onto a plate lined with paper towel. Set them aside to cool, then dust them in cinnamon sugar and cut a slit in the side, ready for filling.

For the custard
Combine the milk and saffron in a heavy based saucepan, and bring to a simmer over a medium heat. Meanwhile, whisk together the egg yolks and sugar, until slightly pale. Add the flour and whisk to combine. Pour the milk over the egg mixture, whisking constantly as you go to avoid scrambling the eggs.

Return the custard to the pan and cook over a low heat for around 5 mins, stirring constantly to avoid burning. Alternate between using a whisk and a spatula – the whisk helps to mix everything together thoroughly and get rid of any lumps as they appear; the spatula is good for scraping the sides and base of the pan, to stop any spots catching. This results in a smooth, consistent custard with no risk of scorching.

The custard will become thick, and just start to bubble. As soon as this happens, remove it from the heat and pour into a clean container. Lay a piece of plastic wrap over the top to avoid a skin forming, then refrigerate to cool completely.

For the pistachios
Mix together the water and sugar in a small heavy based or copper pan, and heat to 114-117°C. When it reaches temperature, remove from the heat and add the pistachios. Stir constantly with a wooden spoon until they are well coated – the surface will whiten as if they were covered with icing sugar. Spread them out onto a tray to cool.

Photography by @bonniesavage
Styling by @charlieduffy__

PISTACHIO BUTTER AND JAM BABKA

Donated by Joel Braham of The Good Egg
@thegoodegg_

"So many innocent people have lost their lives or their loved ones in this devastating conflict. #BakeForSyria is a fantastic way not only of raising awareness and vital funds for the plight of the Syrian people, but also celebrating the country and its cuisine's bold flavours, which continue to influence and inspire what I make in the kitchen."

Babka dough
2 large eggs
120g milk
25g caster sugar
25g honey
420g strong flour
18g fresh yeast
5g table salt
170g butter

PBJ Filling
140g green pistachios
140g purple pistachios
3g ground cinnamon
1 pinch Maldon sea salt
30g honey
300g cherry jam or just your favourite jam
5g sumac
100g fresh cherries

Finishing
50g water
50g caster sugar
rose petals to decorate

When I was thinking about this recipe, I was drawn to the idea of marrying a widely known and classic Jewish treat with the textures and flavours of a traditional Damascene meal. While researching ideas I discovered Sliha, which Damascan Jews eat as a celebratory breakfast dish when a baby's first tooth appears. This discovery fired my imagination, as typical Syrian desserts have two key flavour profiles: syrupy sweetness and roasted nuttiness. The Sliha would provide the right balance of nuttiness with the texture of toasted buckwheat and nuts, offsetting the syrupy sweetness of the candied pumpkin.

For the dough, put the eggs, milk, sugar, honey, flour and yeast in the order listed into a stand mixer with a dough hook attachment. Knead for 2 mins on the lowest speed. Add the salt and increase the speed to 2 for 3 mins.

Add the butter slowly and knead until the dough is elastic and shiny, then prove the dough for 4-5 hours overnight in the fridge.

Add the sugar and water to a small saucepan and heat while whisking until the sugar is dissolved to make the sugar syrup. Allow to cool.

For the pistachio butter blitz the pistachios, cinnamon, sea salt and honey in a food processor, saving some green pistachios for decoration.

Take out your babka dough and roll out to a 45x55cm rectangle.
With a palette knife or spatula spread the pistachio butter all the way to the edges of the dough.
Spread the jam over the pistachio butter layer and scatter over the halved and pitted cherries and sumac. Tightly roll up the babka.

Split into two lengthways, cross the two pieces over each other and twist both ends around the other to shape your babka. Transfer to a parchment lined loaf tin and proof for another 2-3 hours.
Bake at 155 °C for 1 hour 15 mins.
Pour over sugar syrup as soon as it comes out the oven, and top with the reserved crushed green pistachios and rose petals. Allow to cool for at least an hour before slicing.

Photography by @clerkenwellboyec1
Styling by Clerkenwell Boy

BAHARAT DOUGHNUTS AKA PILLOWS OF JOY

Donated by Justin Gellatly of Bread Ahead
@justingellatly

"It is such a great and important cause to get involved in. It harnesses the power of cooking and baking and it is a privilege to be a part of it."

Makes 20 doughnuts

The doughnut dough
500g strong white flour
60g caster sugar
10g fine sea salt
15g fresh yeast
5 eggs
zest of 1 lemon
150g water
Zest of 1 orange
15g Baharat spice mix
125g softened unsalted sugar

Cooking
sunflower oil for deep frying

Tossing
caster sugar

I started baking doughnuts many years ago but I am always trying to come up with new fillings and flavours, so this was a perfect opportunity to get the brain cells working. A doughnut is a great vehicle for Syrian flavours. I have always liked the Baharat spice and I use it a lot to spice lamb, breads and cakes so I wanted to make it a big part of the doughnut.

For the Doughnuts
Place all the ingredients for the dough (apart from the butter) in the bowl of an electric mixer. Using the beater attachment, mix on a medium speed for 6-8 mins or until the dough starts to come away from the sides and form a ball.

Then turn off the mixer and let the dough rest for 1 minute.

Start the mixer again on a medium speed and slowly add the butter to the dough 25g at a time. Once the butter is all incorporated, mix on high speed for a couple of mins until the dough is glossy, smooth and elastic when pulled, then cover the bowl with cling film and prove until it has doubled in size. Knock back the dough, re-cover and put in the fridge to chill overnight.

Take the dough out the fridge and cut in 50g pieces and roll them into smooth, taut buns and place onto a floured baking tray. Leave plenty of room between them as you don't want them to stick together as they prove. Cover lightly with cling film and leave to prove for around 3-4 hours or until they have doubled in size.

Get your deep fat fryer ready or get a heavy based saucepan and fill up ½ way with sunflower oil. Heat the oil to 180°C.

When the oil is heated to 180°C carefully remove the doughnuts from the tray by using a floured pastry scraper and place into the oil. Do not overcrowd the fryer. Fry for 2 mins on each side until golden brown, then remove from fryer and place on some kitchen towel. Toss them in caster sugar while still warm from the fryer, making sure that you cover all of the doughnut in sugar.

Repeat until all fried, but make sure the oil temperature is correct each time you fry.

To fill the doughnut, make a hole in the crease of the doughnut. Fill the piping bag pipe in the doughnut until swollen. Roughly 20-50g is the optimum quantity. Garnish with rose, pistachio and honeycomb.

See next page for filling and toppings

Photography by @KatieWilsonFoto
Styling by @lily_vanilli_cake

ROSE PETAL & PISTACHIO HONEYCOMB AND TOASTED SESAME & CHOCOLATE CUSTARD

Donated by Justin Gellatly of Bread Ahead
@justingellatly

"It is such a great and important cause to get involved in. It harnesses the power of cooking and baking and it is a privilege to be a part of it."

Honeycomb

Note: you will need a thermometer for this recipe.

Makes enough to fill 2 large clip jars and the honeycomb will keep for 2 months. It's great sprinkled on ice cream or dipped in chocolate.

535g caster sugar

66g water

100g pure honey

186g liquid glucose

53g bicarbonate of soda

10 rose petals (sliced thin)

50g chopped green pistachios

Toasted Sesame & Chocolate Custard

Makes enough to fill 20 doughnuts generously

5 tbsp toasted sesame seeds

1 litre full fat milk

30g cocoa powder

12 egg yolks

120g caster sugar

70g plain white flour

150g plain chocolate 70%+ (chopped or buttons)

250ml double cream

25g caster sugar

Honeycomb

Line your largest roasting tray with baking paper.

Put the sugar, water, honey and glucose into a large saucepan, stir together and then on a medium heat, slowly dissolve the sugar into the other ingredients.

Once dissolved, turn up the heat and bring to a rolling boil, then bring the temperature to 145°C. While it's coming up to temperature, get a large whisk ready, then sieve the bicarbonate of soda into a small bowl and be poised ready for it to reach temperature.

Once the sugar mixture reaches 145°C, add all at once the bicarbonate of soda and whisk together in the boiling sugar.

It will start to rise out of the saucepan, so as soon as you have whisked (we are talking seconds here) pour into your lined baking tray, then put on a cooling rack and leave for 30 sec before sprinkling with sliced rose petals and chopped green pistachios.

Once it has cooled and hardened, go kung fu on it and break it into pieces then top your doughnuts.

Toasted Sesame & Chocolate Custard

Put milk, cocoa powder and 4tbsp of toasted sesame in a heavy based saucepan and bring slowly to the boil to infuse the cocoa.

Meanwhile place the egg yolks and sugar in a bowl and mix together for a few seconds, then sieve the flour in and mix together again.

Pour the boiling milk over the yolk mixture, whisking constantly to prevent curdling, and then return the mixture to the saucepan and add the chocolate. Cook over a medium heat, whisking constantly for around 3 mins until nice and thick and all the chocolate has dissolved into the custard

Pass through a fine sieve and place a sheet of cling film on the surface of the custard to prevent a skin from forming.

Leave to the custard to cool and then refrigerate.

Whip the cream and sugar together with the toasted sesame seeds until thick then fold through the chilled custard.

PASTRY & DOUGHS

Photography by @KatieWilsonFoto
Styling by @lily_vanilli_cake

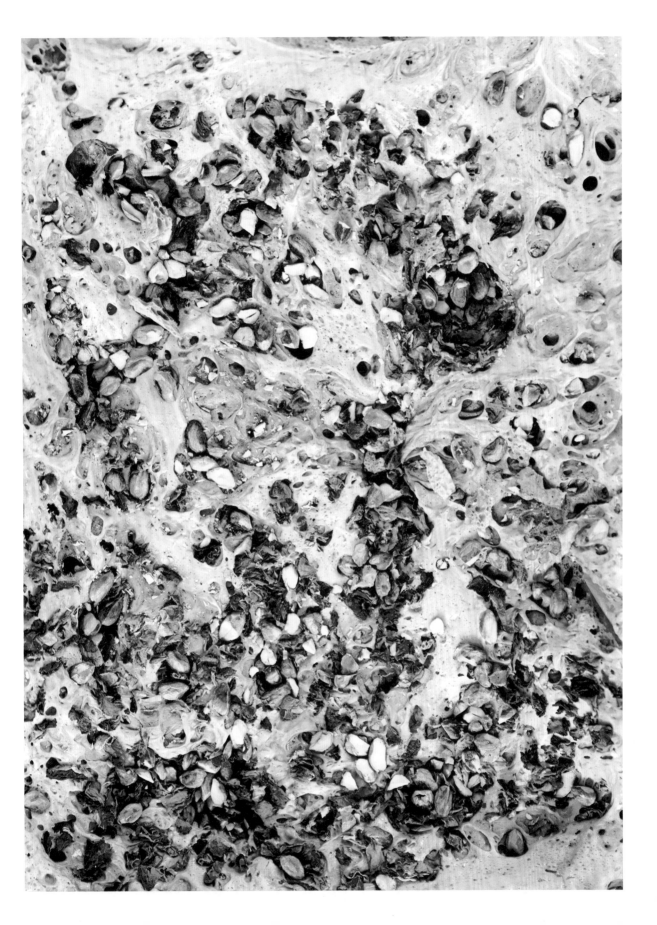

FIG, FETA & ALMOND TART GF

Donated by Melissa Hemsley
@melissa.hemsley

"I adore Syrian food and through working with Team #CookForSyria I have been able to enjoy learning so much about Syrian flavours, ingredients and the Syrian love of sharing food."

For the pastry case

375g ground almonds

2 tsp sea salt

½ tsp bicarb soda

30g butter at room temp

2 medium eggs, organic free range if possible

For the filling

1 tbsp butter

1 large (red) onion, finely sliced

2 fat garlic cloves, finely diced

5 eggs, organic free range if possible

250ml almond milk or regular milk

100g cherry tomatoes, halved

1 large handful fresh parsley

1 tsp dried thyme or oregano / rosemary or 1 tbsp fresh

1 tsp sumac

Sea salt & black pepper, to taste

125g feta

4 medium figs, halved

This fig, feta and almond tart is one of my favourite new dishes to make and share with loved ones. I love it served warm with a big, tangy lemony pile of dressed green leaves or eaten the next day as a snack. Because of the almond pastry case, it's also naturally gluten-free. If you're not a confident pastry maker, don't worry as it's a breeze to make. Everyone loves this tart so double the recipe to make two tarts and give one as a present!

Mix the pastry ingredients by hand to form a dough and then roll into a 3mm-thick disc between two sheets of baking parchment. Line a 24cm-diameter ceramic flan dish or tart tin with the almond pastry, trimming away any excess. Line the pastry case with greaseproof paper, fill with baking beans and chill in the fridge for 20 mins.

Preheat oven to fan 180°C.

Put the bean-filled, chilled tart case in the oven to bake for 10 mins, then remove the baking beans and paper and cook for a further 10 mins until slightly browned. Set aside and reduce the oven temperature to fan 170°C.

Meanwhile, gently fry onion in the butter in a large pan for about 12-15 mins until caramelised. Add the garlic to cook for the final few mins.

In a large bowl, whisk together the eggs and almond milk, add the onion and most of the crumbled feta (saving a little extra for topping) before seasoning with salt and pepper, thyme and sumac.

Pour the egg mixture into your pre-baked tart case. Top with the halved cherry tomatoes and halved figs (cut side up) and push them down slightly. Crumble over the remaining feta and a sprinkling of parsley and cook for 35 mins until golden brown on top and just set in the middle. Allow to cool for 15 mins before diving in.

Photography by @sarahmalcs
Styling by @kittycolescooks

HALVA & FIG BAKED BRIOCHE WITH LABNEH

Donated by Izy Hossack
@izyhossack

"One of my favourite things about food is its ability to bring people together and spark joy. This is exactly what #CookForSyria and #BakeForSyria have done all whilst raising money to support the children affected by the war in Syria. They've been amazingly inspiring projects to be involved in and I've loved learning more about Syrian cuisine too."

Halva frangipane
150g plain sesame halva
50g unsalted butter, softened
1 large egg
¼ tsp salt
1 tsp vanilla extract
50g plain white flour

Syrup
Juice and zest of 1 orange
Juice of 1 lemon
50g granulated sugar
50ml water

Assembly
4-6 slices of brioche
2 tbsp roughly chopped almonds
4-6 ripe figs, thinly sliced
labneh, to serve

If you've ever had bostock before, you'll know how this recipe came to be. Usually a French breakfast pastry made using day-old brioche, it's a pretty decadent start to the day. A layer of frangipane sits on syrup-soaked brioche which is sprinkled with flaked almonds and baked. This is a twist on that dish using Syrian-inspired ingredients of halva, figs and labneh. It's casual enough to be had for breakfast but is special enough that it could also be served as a dessert (especially if you fold some whipped cream into that labneh...).

Preheat the oven to 180°C (or 160°C fan).

In a food processor combine the halva, butter, egg, salt and vanilla extract. Blend until smooth then add the flour and blend again to combine.

In a small pot combine the orange juice and zest, lemon juice and zest, sugar and water. Stir over a medium heat until the sugar has dissolved and the liquid starts to bubble.

Arrange the slices of brioche on a baking tray or two. Use a pastry brush to brush the citrus syrup over the brioche.

Divide the halva frangipane between the brioche slices, spreading it out over each slice in an even layer. Sprinkle with the chopped almonds and bake for 12-15 mins until golden on top.

Arrange the fig slices over the brioche and return to the oven for a further 3-5 mins to soften the figs.

Serve the baked brioche slices warm from the oven with dollops of labneh to balance the sweetness.

Photography by @izyhossack

TAHINI AND CARDAMOM BUNS

Donated by Claire Ptak of Violet Cakes
@violetcakeslondon

"I got involved with #BakeForSyria because the stories I kept hearing and reading about really touched me. I was especially moved by the story of an underground library which provided a calm and quiet refuge for civilians in Daraya, Damascus during the bombing. I hope our book brings some relief to those suffering as a result of the ongoing conflict."

Serves 12

For the filling

250g light brown sugar

1 tbsp ground cardamom

25g unsalted butter, melted plus more to butter the tin

75g tahini

2 tbsp sesame seeds

100g caster sugar for dipping

Zest of 1 orange

For the buns

560g plain flour

2 tbsp baking powder

2 tsp fine sea salt

2 tsp ground cardamom

240g unsalted butter cut into small cubes

300g cold milk

I love baking with Middle Eastern flavours because they are so fragrant, delicate and can be both subtle and bold at once. Inspired by some of my favourite flavours found in the Syrian kitchen, I adapted my classic cinnamon bun for the first #BakeForSyria sale. The subtle bitterness of crushed sesame seeds combined with the sweet warm spice of cardamom bakes into a delightful hybrid of a breakfast treat.

Heat the oven to 180° Fan. Butter the cups of a 12-cup deep muffin tray.

Melt the butter. Mix the light brown sugar and cardamom together until there aren't any lumps and set aside. Weigh out the tahini and sesame seeds and set aside. Weigh out the sugar into a separate bowl and zest the orange into it. Stir to combine and set aside.

Now make the dough. Combine all of the dry ingredients with the cold, cubed butter in a mixing bowl to coarse meal. Slowly add cold milk while the mixer is running until the dough forms into a ball and comes away from the bowl. Turn the dough out onto a lightly floured surface and leave to rest for a few mins. Fold the dough gently over itself once or twice to pull it all together. Let the dough rest a second time.

Heat the oven to 200°C. Clear a large surface, dust lightly with more flour, and roll out the dough out into a large rectangle until about 5mm thick. Brush the surface of the dough with the melted butter and before the butter hardens, sprinkle the cardamom sugar onto the butter. You want a good slightly thick layer. Drizzle evenly with the tahini.

Now roll the dough up away from you, keeping it neat and tight, from bottom (side closest to you) to top. Gently tug the dough towards you as you roll it into a spiral moving away from you, starting in the middle and moving outwards. Once it's all rolled up, gently squeeze the roll to ensure it's the same thickness throughout. Use a sharp knife to slice the roll crossways into 12 even portions. Take a slice of the roll, peel back about 5cm of the loose end of the pastry and fold in back under the bun to loosely cover the bottom. Place into cupcake trays, flap-side down. Scatter with sesame seeds.

Bake for 25 mins

As soon as they're out, flip over onto a wire cooling rack, so that they don't stick to the trays. Dip each bun into the bowl of orange sugar and serve.

Photography by @CharlotteHuCo
Styling by @lily_vanilli_cake

ROSE AND PISTACHIO BOSTOCK

Donated by Dominique Ansel of Dominique Ansel Bakery
@dominiqueansel

"I first met Clerkenwell Boy in Australia, and he told me about the wonderful initiative he and Serena had developed. It's such a great cause and a way to bring together chefs from all over London and all over the world. To give back by sharing what we create with our community is something that's very important to me and to our team."

Makes 8-10 Bostock

For the brioche
325g bread flour

8g salt

39g sugar

5g dry yeast

211g eggs

16g milk

195g unsalted butter, cold, cut into small dice

egg wash (1 egg + 20ml milk, beaten)

For the pistachio cream
367g ground almonds

232g unsalted butter, softened

19g whole eggs

17g pistachio paste

232g granulated sugar

For the rose syrup
21g rose water

213g granulated sugar

1 vanilla bean, sliced lengthwise, seeds scraped

500g water

To serve
rose water

200g chopped pistachios

crystallized rose petals

icing sugar

For each of our menus around the world we create pastries that are just for that city; inspired by the local ingredients, people and traditions. For London, our bostock (a traditional French pastry made with brioche that's soaked with simple syrup and topped with almond frangipane) was inspired by Middle Eastern flavors of roasted pistachios and rose water. So this version is soaked with a light rose water syrup, and instead of almond we use a pistachio frangipane, topped with roasted pistachios and a candied rose leaf on top.

In a stand mixer with a dough hook, combine bread flour, salt, sugar, dry yeast, eggs and milk on medium speed until the dough pulls away from the sides and a smooth ball has formed (12-15 mins). Add butter piece by piece, mixing on medium until the butter is incorporated. The dough should be very smooth and shiny.
Lightly grease a medium bowl with nonstick spray. Transfer the dough to the bowl and cover with cling film pressed directly to the surface, to prevent a skin from forming. Refrigerate overnight.
The next day, shape the dough into a ball and place into a greased loaf pan. Cover with cling film pressed directly onto the surface, and proof the dough at room temperature until doubled in size. Brush the surface of the dough with egg wash, making sure it's completely coated.

Pre-heat oven to 165°C. Bake on a sheet tray on the center rack for 25-30 mins (until the top is golden brown). Remove from oven, cool for 10 mins, then unmold the brioche from the loaf pan, and cool completely.

Pistachio cream
In a stand mixer with a paddle attachment, cream together the butter, eggs, and sugar on medium speed for 3 mins until light and fluffy. Add the ground almonds and pistachio, and mix until smooth. Transfer to a piping bag. Store in the fridge until ready to use.

Rose syrup
Bring all ingredients to a boil in a medium pot, stirring until sugar is dissolved. Remove from heat, and let cool completely.

To serve
Pre-heat oven to 160°C.
Slice the fully-cooled brioche into 2cm-thick slices. brush the slices generously with rose syrup.
Place on a baking sheet lined with parchment.
Pipe a layer of pistachio cream onto the tops of each brioche slice. Sprinkle a handful of chopped pistachios around the edge of the pistachio cream.
Bake for 10 mins (until the pistachio cream is lightly golden on top). Remove from oven and let cool. Finish with a dusting of icing sugar and crystallised petals.

Photography by @CharlotteHuCo
Styling by @lily_vanilli_cake
Portait by @tschauer

ROSE AND HAWAIJ KNOTS

Donated by Benjamina Ebuehi
@bakedbybenji

"I got involved in #BakeForSyria because it's an incredible and much-needed initiative. It's so encouraging to see the ways in which food and baking can be used to provide a unique way of raising awareness about an important issue. It's a real joy to be able to use your skills for something bigger than yourself."

Makes 12

For the dough
300ml whole milk
60g unsalted butter
1 tsp vanilla bean paste
500g bread flour
7g instant yeast
60g caster sugar
½ salt
2 eggs, beaten, one for glazing

For the hawaij filling
1 tbsp ground ginger
1 ½ tsp ground cinnamon
1 tbsp cardamom, from green pods, crushed
pinch ground cloves
¼ tsp ground nutmeg
100g unsalted butter, softened
125g light brown sugar

For the glaze
100g caster Sugar
2 tsp rose water

To decorate
dried rose petals
pearl sugar

Hawaij is a beautifully fragrant and warming spice mix traditionally added to coffee. I love a classic cinnamon roll but using hawaij makes a great change and means I get to use all my favourite spices at once! The delicate rose complements these knots wonderfully, making them truly irresistible.

Gently heat the milk, butter and vanilla in a small saucepan until the butter melts. Leave to cool slightly.

In a large bowl, mix together the flour, sugar, yeast and salt. Add in the milk and beaten egg and gradually mix to form a shaggy dough. Knead the dough on a lightly floured surface for about 8-10 mins until it's smooth and elastic. Place the dough in an oiled bowl, cover and leave to rise for about an hour or until doubled in size.

Make the hawaij by mixing all the spices together. Add the hawaij to a small bowl with the softened butter and sugar and mix by hand until smooth.

Turn the risen dough out onto a lightly floured surface and roll out into a large rectangle. Spread the filling evenly across half of the dough and fold the uncovered side over the filling. Use a pizza cutter or sharp knife to cut the dough into strips approximately 2cm wide.

Twist each strip of dough a few times before holding one end between your thumb and index finger. Wrap the dough around your index and middle fingers before bringing it over the top and tucking underneath. Repeat with all the strips and place them on a lined baking tray leaving plenty of space between each knot. Cover loosely with cling film and leave to rise again for about 45 mins until puffy.

Preheat the oven to Gas Mark 6/200°C. Brush the buns with beaten egg and bake for 18-20 mins until golden brown.

While they're baking, make the glaze by boiling the sugar, 100ml water and the rose water for 2-3 mins. Remove the buns from the oven once cooked and brush generally with the glaze, giving two coats. Sprinkle with pearl sugar and dried rose petals.

Photography by @KatieWilsonFoto
Styling by @lily_vanilli_cake

POMEGRANATE AND SESAME TARTS

Donated by Lily Vanilli
@lily_vanilli_cake

"I'm grateful for the opportunity #CookForSyria and now #BakeForSyria has given me to do something to help those affected by a humanitarian crisis which has been heartbreaking to watch unfold while feeling powerless to help. Serena and Clerkenwell Boy came up with a way to turn a lot of people's good will into something that can actually help others, and the project not only raises significant money to help children affected by the war in Syria but endeavours to celebrate Syrian cuisine and culture and create joy."

Makes 12 mini tarts

For the pastry

350g flour

140g icing sugar

1/2 tsp salt

3 tbsp white sesame seeds

215g cold cubed butter

21g egg yolk

3 eggs

For the filling

100ml pomegranate juice

160ml lemon juice

3 eggs

1 yolks

220g caster sugar

0.5 tbsp sea salt

225g butter (cold, cubed)

These tarts are a celebration of some of my favourite Middle Eastern ingredients. Pomegranates and sesame seeds are indispensable to me as a baker and so versatile. You can buy it but I generally squeeze the fruit by hand for the juice in this recipe, just make sure you run everything through a fine sieve to catch all the pith.

For the Pastry

Evenly combine the dry ingredients, then beat with the cold butter in a mixer, until you have a breadcrumb consistency and no lumps.

Gradually add the lightly beaten eggs and yolk, along with the sesame, and mix just to bring the pastry together – it should be slightly sticky but not wet.
Wrap in clingfilm and rest in the fridge at least 2 hours, but preferably overnight.

Preheat oven to 180°C.

Once rested, remove pastry from the fridge until just soft enough to roll, then roll out to around 3mm thickness and cut rounds to fit your tart tins.

Grease and line the tins, trimming any overhanging pastry from the edges, then rest in the fridge again for a minimum of 2 hours.

Now to blind bake: use a piece of baking paper to line each pastry shell and fill it to the brim with baking beans (or a substitute like raw chickpeas).

Bake for 15 mins or until golden brown at the edges and then remove the beans. Bake for another 5 mins or until the pastry is baked a nice even brown.

For the Filling

Cut cold butter into 2cm chunks and place in freezer to chill.

Combine the juices, whole eggs, yolk, sugar, and salt in a pan over a medium heat. Whisk continuously until the mixture becomes very thick (10 to 12 mins). When ready, the whisk will leave a trail when dragged through the mixture.

Remove from the heat and allow to cool just slightly.

Pour your mixture into a bowl or food processor and add the butter 1 chunk at a time, blending after each addition, until it is incorporated, before adding the next piece.

Fill cooled tart shells with the pomegranate mixture and leave to set in the fridge for around 2 hours or until firm.

Photography by @CharlotteHuCo
Styling by @lily_vanilli_cake
Portait by @alice_whitby

TUMERIC & COCONUT 'ROSE' BAKLAVAS

Donated by Lily Vanilli
@lily_vanilli_cake

"I'm grateful for the opportunity #CookForSyria and now #BakeForSyria has given me to do something to help those affected by a humanitarian crisis which has been heartbreaking to watch unfold while feeling powerless to help. Serena and Clerkenwell Boy came up with a way to turn a lot of people's good will into something that can actually help others, and the project not only raises significant money to help children affected by the war in Syria but endeavours to celebrate Syrian cuisine and culture and create joy."

Makes 12

For the baklava

12 sheets of filo pastry

150g butter, melted and cooled

170g sweetened shredded coconut

For the syrup

1 cup water

¾ cup honey

1 tbsp lemon juice

1.5 tbsp grated turmeric

Equipment

a silicone mini cupcake pan

I made a rose shaped baklava (flavoured with rose and walnut) for the #CookForSyria recipe book, but I have tweaked it so much since then that I wanted to share the new one. I now use shredded coconut which gives it a really beautiful texture, turmeric for the syrup and roll them differently so they look much neater. These are quick and easy to make once you get the hang of it, just be a little bit patient at first if you're new to using filo.

For each baklava

Cut each sheet of filo into thirds, keeping them under a damp tea towel so they don't dry out.
Take one piece at a time and lay it out lengthways on your counter.

Brush both sides generously with cooled, melted butter.

Sprinkle with 14g sweetened shredded coconut in the middle of the sheet, evenly all the way across.

Now fold up the bottom and top of the filo sheet over the coconut.

Now roll up your 'rose', left to right, to form a tightly wound spiral.

Place in a generously buttered silicone mini cupcake pan.

Bake for 20-25 mins or until browning and baked.

For the syrup

In a medium saucepan, combine the honey, water, turmeric and lemon.

Bring to a boil over medium/high heat, stirring until honey is dissolved, then reduce heat to low and simmer until syrup has started to thicken.

Brush the syrup over the cooling baklava, then allow everything to cool before serving.

Photography by @CharlotteHuCo
Styling by @lily_vanilli_cake
Portait by @alice_whitby

FIG AND WALNUT GALETTE

Donated by Nadine Ingram of Flour and Stone
@flourandstone

"What we do as bakers is deeply connected to the giving of our time and knowledge in order to love, heal and nourish through food. That sentiment goes hand in hand with this important cause."

Makes 12

Filling

100g sesame seeds

1 tbsp cardamom

100ml honey

300g dried figs, stems removed

200g walnuts, roughly chopped

20ml rose water

100g apricot jam

Zest of 2 lemons and oranges

Pastry

300g plain or whole wheat flour or half-and-half of each.

200g unsalted butter, slightly chilled

100g caster sugar

½ tsp salt

60ml ice water

Glaze for baking

1 tbsp butter, melted

3 tbsp caster or demerara sugar

I was inspired by Nigel Slater's recent jaunt to the Middle East where he went into local people's homes and experienced food as they do. Each family member had a role to play in either harvesting or preparing food and that seemed to reflect a lovely sense of togetherness. I have tried to write a recipe using only flavours that a family living in Syria would. I imagine the sweetness and fragrance of these ingredients has brought great comfort to the Syrian family table over time.

To make the pastry cut the butter into small cubes. Sieve the flour(s) into a bowl with the salt and caster sugar, then mix them roughly together with your hands to combine. Add the butter and rub with the flour between your fingertips to flatten it and form a breadcrumb consistency with some larger flakes of butter throughout. Add the ice water and use your hands to distribute it into the pastry, then press the dough together to form a ball.

Cut into halves, shape roughly into balls and flatten a little to aid the rolling process later. Cover with plastic wrap and rest in the fridge for 1 hour.

Meanwhile prepare the filling by toasting the sesame seeds in a dry fry pan over medium heat until they are golden, then set them aside. Crush the cardamom pods. Place honey into a small saucepan on the stove, add the cardamom (pods and all) and bring gently to the boil to infuse. Set aside to cool. Once cooled, strain to remove the cardamom.

Place figs into a food processor and puree them coarsely. Scrape into a bowl and fold through the walnuts, sesame seeds, rose water, apricot jam, honey and zest evenly.

Line a 35cm square baking sheet with baking paper, then remove the pastry rounds from the fridge. Dust the benchtop lightly with flour and place one of the pastry rounds in the center of the flour. Sprinkle the top of the dough with a little more flour and roll it out to a diameter of 30cm with an even surface.

Transfer the first pastry round onto the prepared baking sheet and rest in the fridge for 15 mins.

Then spread the filling over the base of the pastry leaving a 2cm border all the way around the outside. Build it up into a slightly domed shape and use an offset palette knife or spatula to smooth over the filling. This process can also be done with a piping bag (if you have one) by spiraling the filling over the pastry base.

Set the galette aside and roll out the other pastry round in the same way as the first, transferring it directly onto the top of the filling once you have done so. Trim the edges neatly, remembering to leave a 1cm border of pastry all the way around. At this stage you can leave the border plain or crimp the edges to form a scalloped detail as I have done here.

Rest the galette for 15 mins in the fridge and preheat the oven to 180°C.

Decorate the top of the galette by using a small sharp knife to score patterns in the pastry. Brush the galette with the melted butter and some sugar.

Bake for 50 mins or until dark golden.

Serve hot or cold.

PASTRY & DOUGHS Photography by @nikkito

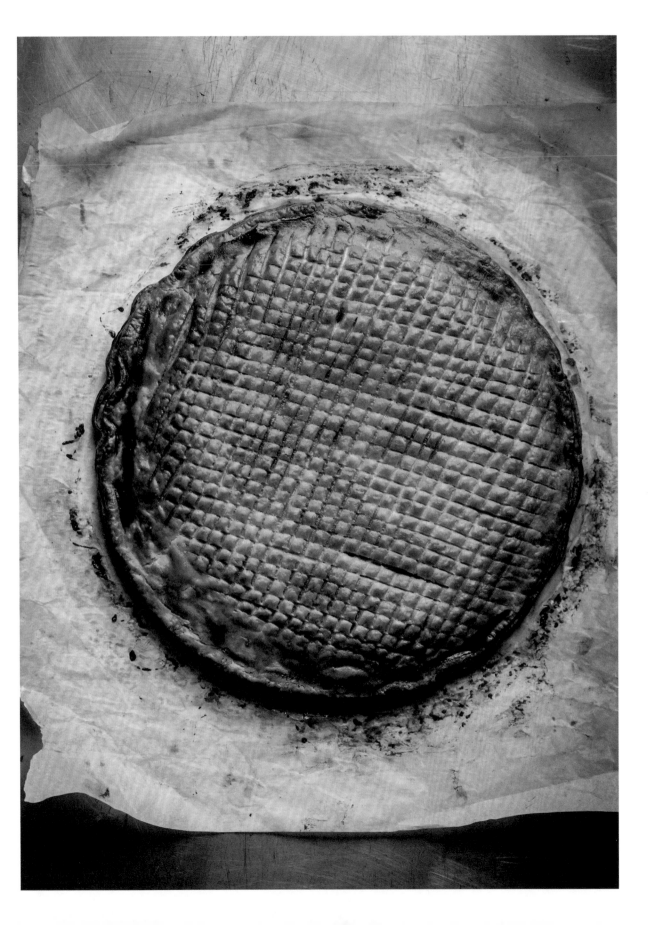

LINZETORTE

Donated by Lizzie Parle and Matthew Doran of Railroad
@railroadhackney

"It's really exciting that the London food scene is branching out and having a social impact on an international scale. Running a food business in London can be hard and competitive, but collaborative projects like #BakeForSyria can help us collectively shift our perspective and efforts towards something more meaningful. For people like us who are constantly drawing inspiration from Middle Eastern cooking and culture, this feels like the right way celebrate it and give something back."

Serves 10

For the pastry

250g unsalted butter

250g whole blanched almonds, finely ground

250g caster sugar

250g plain flour, plus extra for dusting

¼ tsp baking powder

Pinch of salt

2-3 egg yolks

For the filling

400g loquats (nespole), stoned weight

100g redcurrants and/or raspberries

1-2 tbsp caster sugar (depending on how

sweet/tart your fruit is)

1tsp orange blossom water

1 squeeze of lemon juice

Egg wash

2 tbsp milk

1 egg yolk

To serve

lightly whipped double cream or crème fraîche

You will need

30cm fluted tart case with a removable base.

Baking beans to blind bake the pastry base.

This Linzertorte is a departure from the original Austrian jam filled tart, but the characteristic nut-filled pastry and lattice remain. Loquats (also known as nespole) are like a cross between a plum and an apricot. They are among the first fruits of Spring, often found at Turkish, Middle Eastern or Chinese Grocers. Their mild, creamy flesh works really well with orange blossom water.

Recipe adapted from the Railroad cookbook

180C

Place almonds, sugar, flour, baking powder and salt into a food processor and mix to combine. Add chilled butter and pulse to resemble breadcrumbs. Add two of the egg yolks and pulse. If it looks like the pastry is dry, add another egg yolk and pulse. When it has come together, turn out and bring together with your hands. Divide into two equal parts, wrap in cling film, and squash to make 2 thick disks. Chill in the fridge for at least 1 hour.

Remove the pastry from the fridge 20 mins before rolling it out—this will allow it to soften up slightly. Flour the bench and your rolling pin. Roll one pastry disk and to a round about 3cm wider than the tart shell.

Transfer to the tin, push into the corners and trim the edges. Leave it in the fridge for now.

Roll out the second piece of pastry the same as the first—then cut into long strips about 2.5cm wide. Place them onto a lined baking sheet, cover and refrigerate until needed.

Line the cooled tart shell with greaseproof paper, fill with baking beans and bake for 10 mins, then remove beans and bake until golden brown. Remove to cool.

Slice the loquats into quarters and toss with orange blossom water and a tablespoon of sugar. Fill the cool pastry shell with the loquats and scatter the redcurrants and raspberries over the top. Top with the pastry lattice and brush with the egg wash. Bake for 35-45 mins until baked.

Cool and serve with crème fraîche or lightly whipped cream.

Photography by @CharlotteHuCo
Styling by @lily_vanilli_cake

DATE TART WITH HINT OF ORANGE

Donated by Terri Mercieca of Happy Endings
@happyendingsldn

"#BakeForSyria and #CookForSyria are wonderful ways to give aid in a complex situation. I want to use my skills as a pastry chef to help raise money for children living in dire conditions that are completely out of their control. I chose this dish because what I wish for them is the warmth, comfort and sweetness that they deserve as little ones."

I've been making versions of this date tart since I first became a pastry chef. I love it because it's rich and intense but brings a real sense of warmth and comfort. For this version, I've combined a traditional English dessert with the richness, spice and natural sweetness of Syrian cooking. The Medjool dates, combined with a spice-mix laden with black pepper and orange are a real winner in this silky custard tart!

For the pastry

120g plain flour

60g unsalted butter

40g pure icing sugar

15g almond flour

1 organic or free-range egg (50g)

1g Maldon sea salt

Date and orange jam

100g fresh medjool dates

50g orange juice freshly squeezed and strained

Black 4 spice

7g black pepper

1g cloves

0.5g ground cinnamon

1g freshly grated nutmeg

Custard tart mix

5 organic or free-range egg yolks

420 g double cream

55g caster sugar

1 orange rind only

5g black 4 spice mix

Fresh Dates

6 fresh dates, pitted and cut in half lengthways

To make the pastry shell
Dice cold the butter to 3mm cubes and chill. Sift the flour and icing sugar into a bowl, then add the almond flour and salt. Remove the chilled butter from the fridge and add to the flour mix. With your fingers, rub the butter into the flour mix until you have a sandy texture. Add the egg and bring the dough together gently with your hands. Then knead just a little to achieve a smooth dough. Rest in the fridge for 2 hours. Remove and soften at room temp until it's easy to roll. On a lightly floured surface, roll to no more than 3mm thick. Place carefully in the tart shell. Now freeze the tart shell to rest it.

Preheat the oven to 170°C. Fill your tart shell with a double layer of cling film, then raw rice, place in the oven and bake until nicely golden brown at the edges, remove the rice, return to the oven and bake for a further 5 to 7 mins. Take 1 beaten egg and brush all over the tart shell and place back in the oven just briefly until its golden, then remove and cool.

Date and orange jam
Pit and dice the dates, place in a small saucepan with the orange juice and cook on a low heat until the mix comes together.

Black 4 spice
Take all the spices together and grind until a fine powder. Sieve to remove the chunky bits

Custard tart mix
Bring cream to the boil with the black 4 spices, once boiled, remove from heat, cover with cling film and allow to infuse for 30 mins. In a steel bowl, whisk the egg yolks and the caster sugar together. Bring the cream back to the boil and pour onto the egg and sugar mix, gently whisking in. Strain the mixture through a fine sieve. If there is a lot of foam on top, use a spoon to remove it and discard.

Assembly
Preheat oven to 120 degrees In the baked shell, spread the date jam over the bottom in an even layer. Cut dates in half lengthways, pit them, and arrange over the date jam. Pour custard into the shell, almost to the top. Sift remaining spice mix over it, place in the oven, and top up with more custard. Bake for approximately 1 hour or until there is slight wobble in the centre. Cool completely.

Photography by @KatieWilsonFoto
Styling by @lily_vanilli_cake
Portrait by @gmotophotos

BLACKBERRY, CARDAMOM & ROSE MAHALABI BRÛLÉE TART

Donated by Safia Shakarchi
@dearsafia

"Being involved in #BakeForSyria has been an amazing adventure. Using my sweet treats to give back to a region to which I owe a lot of who I am is a small but special contribution, which I feel lucky to make. A sweet tooth has no borders, and I hope that this book allows us to better understand that beautiful part of the world."

Makes 12 individual 10cm tarts,
Or one large 35cm rectangular tart

For the pastry
250g plain flour

125g caster sugar

125g unsalted butter, cold and cubed

1 egg, lightly beaten

1 egg white, lightly beaten

For the mahalabi filling
(this can also be made as a standalone dessert in cups or one larger dish)

750ml almond milk

60g cornflour

60ml maple syrup

1 tsp ground cardamom

3 tbsp rose water

For the topping
100g demerara sugar

150g blackberries

squeeze of lemon juice

handful slivered pistachios

Whilst at times it was confusing growing up between Arabic and British cultures, I have always been certain about my love for Middle Eastern flavours; they have shaped my style of baking. The filling here is inspired by my grandmother's mahalabi, a delicious rose water and cardamom pudding, and the tart itself by the love of French patisserie that she passed onto me.

For the pastry
Place flour, sugar and butter in the bowl of a food processor and pulse to resemble breadcrumbs. Add the beaten egg and pulse until it comes together to form a dough. Turn onto a clean surface, wrap in cling film and flatten to a circle. Refrigerate for at least one hour.

Remove 10 mins before you use it. Take a small piece and on a lightly floured surface, roll it into a circle about 12-15cm wide and 3mm thick. Press gently into the base and edges of your tart tin. Trim the excess and repeat with the remaining dough. Prick the base of each and freeze for 20 mins.

Preheat oven to 180°C. Line each tart case with cling film, fill with baking beans and blind bake for 12 mins. Remove baking beans and bake for a further 12 mins until golden brown. Brush with a little beaten egg white and bake another minute to seal. Remove and cool completely.

For the mahalabi filling
Place 650ml almond milk in a small pan with the syrup and cardamom. In a mug, combine 100ml almond milk with the cornflour to form a paste. Add to the saucepan and bring mixture to the boil, whisking gently.

Reduce heat slightly, add rose water and continue whisking until mixture thickens to a custard-like consistency. Fill cooled tart cases to the top. Alternatively, pour into individual cups or a large dish if making as a standalone dessert. Set aside to come to room temperature and refrigerate until set (about 4 hours, ideally overnight).

For the topping
Sprinkle the tops with demerara sugar and spread to cover. Using a blowtorch, carefully caramelize the sugar. Refrigerate for no more than an hour to ensure the sugar stays crisp.

Pop blackberries in a small pan with lemon juice and 1tbsp water, heating until juices turn a dark purple and blackberries soften but keep their shape. Top each tart or cup with a spoonful of blackberries, finish with pistachios, and serve immediately.

Photography by @KatieWilsonFoto
Styling by @dearsafia
Portrait by @ryelondon

NUT AND ROSE WATER TART

Donated by Ollie Gold and Florin Grama of Pophams Bakery
@pophamsbakery

"Ollie: I was incredibly lucky to grow up with a loving and generous family who raised me with an understanding of the beauty of giving. It was one of my dreams when starting a new business to create a platform that would enable me to give back. The fact we can do this through #BakeForSyria means a lot. The Syrian people are desperate for help – children the most – and they deserve a life like every one of us."

For the honey syrup

300g sugar

200g honey

180ml water

20ml rose water

5 cloves

4 star anise

4 cardamom pods

2 medium size cinnamon sticks

For the filling

240g ground almonds

180g walnuts, fine chopped

40g pistachio, fine chopped

40g pistachio paste

200ml honey syrup

60ml rose water

For the pastry base

180g shredded filo dough

75g butter, melted

10ml rose water

For the garnish

pistachio

rose petals

Florin: I lived in Cyprus for four years, surrounded by food and desserts flavoured with spice and soaked in syrups and very much influenced by the Middle East. This opened me up to a new and exquisite understanding of food which translated into my own cooking and baking. I have loved nuts since childhood and wanted to combine both these elements.

For the syrup
Combine all the ingredients together in a small saucepan. Bring to boil, set to a medium low heat and simmer for 5 mins. Set aside to cool.

For the pastry, combine the shredded filo and melted butter in a bowl and then add rose water. Start to work and break the filo into smaller pieces with your hands until all butter is incorporated.

Preheat the oven 175°C/350°F/Gas mark 4.

Press your mix down into the base of a prepared 20cm tart tin (make sure it is levelled).

Bake for 45-50 mins until golden.

For the filling
Mix all the ingredients well in a bowl, then place it into the baked tart case and return to the oven for 20 mins.

Let it cool down and set overnight, drizzle with honey syrup, then finally add a handful of chopped pistachios and rose petals to garnish.

Can be served with orange marmalade.

Photography by @KatieWilsonFoto
Styling by @lily_vanilli_cake

RHUBARB, GOAT'S CURD & PISTACHIO KNAFEH

Donated by Nicholas Balfe of Salon Brixton
@salon_brixton

"When I first heard about #CookForSyria back in 2016, it immediately struck a chord with me. We are blessed in this country to have such a rich and diverse food culture, and it's heartening to see how it has been used to support those who are less fortunate than we are."

Serves 6-8

500g rhubarb, cleaned and cut into 1cm pieces

100g sugar

1/2 tsp rose water

250g kadayif (shredded filo) pastry

125g butter

Pinch of salt

100g shelled unsalted pistachios

400g goat's curd

100g double cream

100g caster sugar

1/2 tsp rose water

I first encountered knafeh in the Palestinian capital of Ramallah, while travelling in the Middle East. I'd made my way to the city in search of a particular shawarma bar, but I kept coming across street stalls and shops devoted entirely to knafeh. Eventually those glistening, syrup-coated, cheese-filled pastries became too hard to resist. My portion was served warm from the oven and doused in orange and rose scented syrup. It was rich, sweet, gooey and delicious!

My version is lighter and less sweet but hopefully just as tasty. I would recommend using rhubarb if it's in season, since it gives a great acidity. Otherwise, fresh strawberries, raspberries or pomegranate also work. You can usually find kadayif pastry in Middle Eastern grocery shops and supermarkets. If not, just use filo.

First, cook the rhubarb. Preheat the oven to 180°C. Toss the rhubarb and sugar together in a bowl so everything is coated. Transfer to a baking tray, cover with parchment paper and leave to macerate for 20 mins or so. Bake in the oven for 10 mins or until just softening, then set aside, still covered in parchment. Once cool, drain off the syrup with has been produced, and add the rose water. Reduce the syrup by half, so it's slightly thickened.

Next, prepare the pastry. Line two 20cm loaf tins with parchment paper. Melt the butter in a saucepan, then leave on the heat, stirring regularly until it begins to brown. It will smell toasty, caramelly and nutty. Take off the heat and add a pinch of salt. Scrunch up the Kadayif pastry, so the strands break up a bit, then pour over the warm butter. Mix together so all the pastry has been coated in the brown butter. Pack the pastry into the loaf tins, then bake for 15 mins or until golden brown.

Meanwhile, toast the pistachios in the oven for 8 mins, then chop into small pieces.

Finally, make the filling by whipping together the goat's curd, cream, sugar and rose water. A free standing mixer with a K-beater attachment is best, but a hand held whisk or even a wooden spoon would work too.

Assemble the knafeh by spreading the goats curd mixture onto one layer of kadayif pastry. Add the rhubarb, then some of the syrup, then the other layer of pastry. Finally, top with the pistachios and drizzle over the rest of the syrup.

Photography by @CharlotteHuCo
Styling by @lily_vanilli_cake
Portrait by @twilsonphotography

PASTRY & DOUGHS

QUINCE, FIG, ORANGE BLOSSOM, HONEY AND WALNUT TART WITH SPELT AND ALMOND PASTRY

Donated by Henrietta Inman
@henriettainman

"One of the most wonderful things about #CookForSyria is that it hasn't just been about the cooks and bakers involved, but also all the other supporters. Its success shows what can be achieved when hundreds of people work together. Support for this campaign is building day by day and it's amazing and uplifting to imagine what #CookForSyria might achieve next."

Serves 8-12

For the pastry
95g cubed unsalted cold butter

125g white spelt flour

25g ground almonds

¼ tsp sea salt flakes

35g golden caster sugar or coconut sugar

zest ¼ unwaxed orange

1 egg

1 medium egg yolk

For the walnut frangipane
90g walnut halves

110g unsalted butter

80g golden caster sugar or coconut sugar

½ tsp sea salt flakes

finely grated zest ½ unwaxed orange

2 medium eggs

90g ground almonds

For the baked quince
2 large quince, peeled, cored and cut into about ½ cm slices

1 orange, juice and pared zest

3 tbsp light brown muscovado or coconut sugar

3 tbsp honey

½ vanilla pod, optional

For the fig, honey and orange blossom quick jam
blossom jam

225g dried figs, roughly chopped

100g orange juice and finely grated zest ½ unwaxed orange

1 tbsp honey

1 tbsp orange blossom water

I first made this tart for the #CookForSyria pop-up café in London during December 2017. In a way, this dish is what the whole #CookForSyria campaign has been about – not only recreating Syrian dishes but celebrating their flavours and ingredients and marrying them with our own. It's been an incredible year for #CookForSyria, as it's crossed the seas from London to Paris and Sydney, demonstrating the great power of food and culture, how it can unite people, bringing them together to help one another in times of need.

Butter the sides and base of a 23cm (9in) loose-bottomed tart tin.

Make the pastry by mixing together the flour, almonds, salt, sugar and orange zest in a freestanding mixer or bowl. Add the cubes of butter and combine, with the paddle or your fingertips, until the mixture resembles breadcrumbs.
Add the yolk and mix once until it just comes together. If it looks a little dry, add a little of the egg white until it binds. Bring the pastry together in your hands, flatten into a rough 1cm thick circle, wrap in parchment paper and chill for 15 – 30 mins.
Roll the chilled pastry out to 3mm thick, to fit the tin, trimming off excess. Chill in the fridge for 30 mins.

For the frangipane
Preheat the oven to 180C. On a baking tray lined with baking parchment, lightly toast the walnuts in the oven for about 4 mins. Cool, then rough blitz in a food processor. Cream the butter, sugar, salt and orange zest until light and fluffy. Beat the eggs together. Combine the ground almonds with the toasted chopped walnuts. Gradually add the eggs to the butter mixture, alternating with the nuts, until the mix is smooth and homogenous. Line the chilled pastry shell with baking parchment and fill with baking beans or raw rice. Blind bake for 10 mins. Remove the beans or rice and bake for a further 10 mins, or until just golden brown. Brush the baked shell with the extra egg yolk and return to the oven for 1-2 mins, until just dry.
For the quince, place all the ingredients into a baking tray or ovenproof dish, mixing it all up with your hands so that the fruit is coated with the orange juice, sugar and honey. Cover with foil and bake for 20-30 mins until you can pierce a piece of quince all the way through with a sharp knife but there is still a little resistance. Set aside.
Make the fig, orange and honey quick jam. Place all the ingredients, except the orange blossom, in a medium saucepan and bring to the boil. Lower to a simmer until all the juice has been absorbed and you have a figgy paste. Add the orange blossom, mix until just absorbed and remove from the heat.

Spread the fig jam over the baked pastry shell to make an even layer of jam; spread over the frangipane, then the quince slices. Bake for about 20-25 mins, until the edges of the frangipane are golden and the middle is set but with a tiny wobble. Pour off any leftover cooking juices from the quince into a saucepan. Add a little apricot jam or marmalade and bring to the boil, adding a little more honey too if you want. Remove from the heat and add 1-2 tbsp orange blossom water. Use this to glaze the tart with a pastry brush. Cool, decorate and serve!

PASTRY & DOUGHS

Photography by @KatieWilsonFoto
Styling by @henriettainman

OSH EL BULBUL OR BIRD'S NESTS WITH FIGS, ORANGE BLOSSOM YOGHURT CREAM, HONEY AND PISTACHIOS

Donated by Henrietta Inman
@henriettainman

"One of the most wonderful things about #CookForSyria is that it hasn't just been about the cooks and bakers involved, but also all the other supporters. Its success shows what can be achieved when hundreds of people work together. Support for this campaign is building day by day and it's amazing and uplifting to imagine what #CookForSyria might achieve next."

Serves 20

400g kadaifi pastry

100g unsalted butter, melted, plus extra for greasing

200g labneh or Greek yoghurt or goat's curd

200g double cream

2-3 tbsp golden icing sugar, or more to taste

1 tsp cinnamon

3 tbsp orange blossom water, or more to taste

5 tbsp honey

fresh figs or other fresh fruit or berries or quince slices, baked as for the tart I made for this book

When I was researching Syrian baking for the second #BakeForSyria sale in November 2017, I came across Osh El Bulbul—little kadaifi pastry nests baked with butter, filled with pistachios after baking and finished with sugar syrup. I'd only used kadaifi pastry once before and loved how versatile it was, adding a lovely crunch to creamy and fruity puddings. For this recipe, instead of playing with a fruit tart and adding Syrian flavours I decided to add my own twist using figs - but you could use quince or any other fruit you like.

Preheat the oven to 180°C. Grease a large baking tray or ovenproof dish with butter. I use a 35cm round one; you can buy similar round trays in most Middle Eastern and Turkish shops and delis. A square tray is fine too

Lay 400g kadaifi pastry out on a large clean surface. Take a small handful of pastry and start to make nests, wrapping it around your index and middle fingers. One by one, place the nests in the tray, working from the edge to the centre, repeating until the tray is full and the pastry nests are packed tightly together. Pour over the butter, sieve over a 1 tbsp of the icing sugar and cinnamon and bake for about 10-20 mins until crispy and golden brown. Leave to cool.

Whip together the labneh, yoghurt or goat's curd with the cream, remaining icing sugar and half of the orange blossom water. Taste and adjust the sweetness and orange blossom as you like. Bring the honey to a boil with the other half of the orange blossom water and reduce a little. Fill the nests with the cream, then a slice of fig, drizzle over the honey syrup and finish with chopped pistachios and fresh or dried rose petals if you like.

This was inspired by the recipe for Osh el Bulbul in 'Syria, Recipes from Home' by Itam Azzam and Dina Mousawi, published by Trapeze

Extra notes
Both my recipes for this book are really adaptable. You can use different nuts to finish the nests or in the frangipane, rose water instead or orange blossom, other fruits depending on what is in season, or other dried fruits.

Photography by @KatieWilsonFoto
Styling by @lily_vanilli_cake

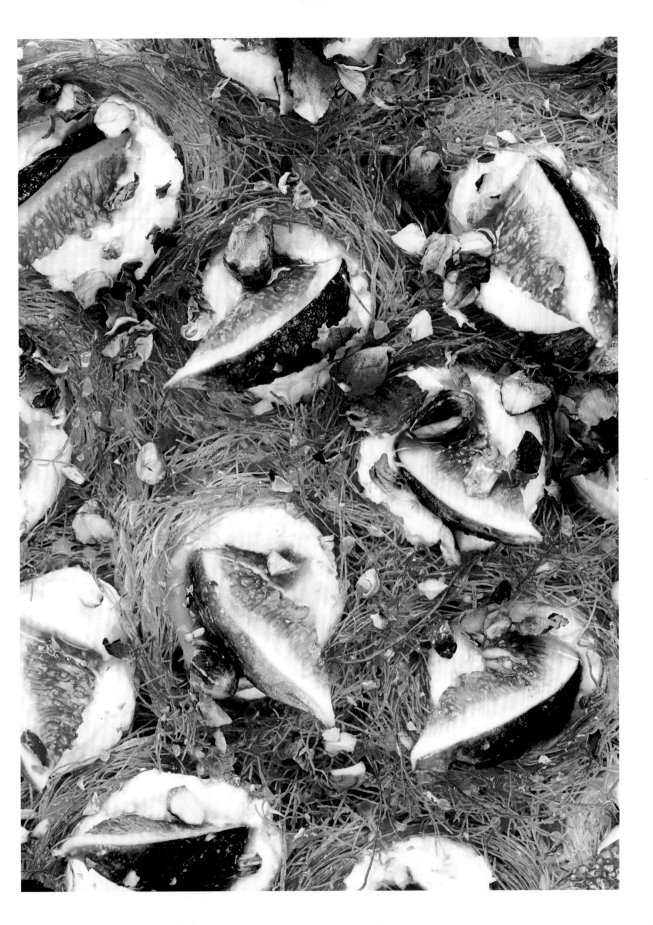

KOLOMPEH

Donated by Bita Fallah of Jacob the Angel
@jacobtheangellondon

"I think #BakeForSyria is a fantastic way to help raise money and awareness for the child victims of the war in Syria, while highlighting all the amazing food the region has to offer."

For the pastry

500g flour

250g ghee

170g yoghurt

2 egg yolks

2/3 tbsp baking powder

1/2 tbsp saffron water (add some hot water to pulverised saffron and leave for 10 mins to extract the colour)

For the filling

160g pitted dates with skins removed

1/2 tsp ground cardamom

1/2 tsp ground cinnamon

60g chopped walnuts

This is a delicious, delicate dish made with no artificial sugar. It consists mainly of dates, walnuts, cardamom and pistachios. It always reminds me of happy childhood days, sunshine, family gatherings and traditional Persian afternoon tea. Different versions of this healthy sweet appear in the cuisines of many Middle Eastern countries, and is also seen today in the west as energy balls, bars, squares and so on. Give it a try and enjoy them with a fresh cup of tea. They will make you happy!

Add the ghee and about half of the flour to a bowl.

Mix in another bowl the baking powder and the yoghurt, then add the egg yolks, followed by the saffron water.

Add the mixture to the dough, and add the remaining flour little by little.

Let it rest for 2 hours in the fridge.

Meanwhile, to make the filling, mash the dates into a paste.

Add the chopped walnuts, cardamom and cinnamon and incorporate into the mixture.

When it is ready, roll out the dough between pieces of cling film, until it's thinner than a coin.

Preheat the oven to 160C.

Cut out rounds from the dough with a scone cutter (dust it in some flour to stop it sticking).

Put a spoonful of filling on a round and place another round on top.

Press the edges together and make a pattern on top of the sweets – In Iran there are special stamps with traditional patterns that are used specifically for this.

Tighten the edges of the kolompeh by rolling around it little by little to create pretty edges.

Put them on an oven tray and bake them for 20 mins at 160C.

Get yourself a cup of tea and enjoy your fresh kolompeh.

Photography by @KatieWilsonFoto
Styling by @lily_vanilli_cake

BAHARAT SPICED FREEKEH, ALMOND & APRICOT FILO PIE

Donated by Selin Kiazim of Oklava
@oklava_ldn

"#CookForSyria and #BakeForSyria are truly remarkable projects. It is an honour to take part and to be able to use food and baking to help make a small positive difference in the lives of vulnerable children in Syria."

Serves 4

100g freekeh, rinsed

50g unsalted butter, room temperature

50g unsalted butter

20ml extra virgin olive oil

1 onion, diced

3 garlic cloves, finely grated

1 heaped tbsp baharat

30g dried apricots, halved, preferably natural

25g whole blanched almonds

16 whole blanched almonds, cut in half lengthwise

6 large sheets of filo pastry, cut in half

25g unsalted butter, melted

flaky sea salt

This is an adaptation of a recipe in my own book which uses rice. Freekeh is a delicious, nutty grain that I thought would work perfectly in the pies with a little perfume from the Baharat. For relatively little effort this is a seriously comforting and impressive recipe that combines amazing textures, tastes and smells in equal measures.

Melt the 50g of butter with olive oil. Add in the onion and almonds, gently caramelise on a medium heat for 10 mins or until golden. Add in the garlic.

Add in all the baharat and apricots, continue to cook for 5 mins on a low heat.

Now add in the freekeh and season with salt and pepper. Make sure you coat the freekeh with everything really well. Cover with water to 1 cm above the freekeh.

Bring the freekeh up to the boil and then turn the heat down to its lowest setting, cover with a lid and cook for 20 mins or until all the water has evaporated and the freekeh is cooked, if it is a little undercooked then add a little more water and continue to cook.

Take out of the pan and spread out onto a tray to completely cool down.

Preheat the oven to 190°C fan.

Use the butter at room temperature to grease 4 ramekin moulds approx. 8cm in diameter.

Place the sliced almonds in a decorative way around the moulds. Place into the freezer for 5 mins to set.

Take 1 mould out of the freezer at a time. Place a sheet of filo carefully into the mould trying to reach all the corners, lightly brush with melted butter. Then, add another 2 sheets of filo, buttering in-between. Fill the ramekin up with the cooled freekeh. Fold in the edges of the pastry into the centre, buttering any overlaps. Press down the top and brush with a little more butter. Repeat the process 3 more times.

Put into the oven for approx. 30 - 45 mins or until golden brown and crisp. Take out of the oven and allow them to rest for 5mins.

Carefully turn out onto a plate. Serve with yoghurt and pomegranate seeds.

KNAFEH

Donated by Sandra Greiss
@sandra.greiss

"I find the initiative incredibly inspiring for many reasons. Food plays a big part in Middle Eastern culture and using it to raise money for a cause that is close to my home and heart means a lot to me. Children are our future and seeing the lives of Syrian children affected by war in their own country is heartbreaking. #CookForSyria not only raises the awareness of what is happening in Syria, it also gives us a chance to try and make a difference."

Serves 30

Sugar Syrup
1 cup of water
2/3 cup of granulated sugar
juice of 1 lemon

Knafeh
600g kataifi, defrosted (shredded pastry, usually found in the frozen section of middle eastern and greek supermarkets)

300g ricotta cheese (you can go up to 500g if you want a lot of filling. We prefer a creamy centre so we used 500g)

600ml single cream
1 tbsp of rose water
2 tbsp of cornflour
1 tbsp caster sugar
1 large knob (150g) of unsalted butter, melted
100ml vegetable oil

Topping
handful of pistachios, chopped
handful of walnuts, chopped
1 tbsp brown sugar
1 tsp of cinnamon

My grandmother played the biggest role in this recipe because her knafeh is my absolute favourite for both its simplicity and its perfection. She used to spend some time in London every couple of years so she passed her recipes on to my aunt, who passed them on to me. When I thought of how to take the best of both worlds and come up with a Syrian and Egyptian knafeh, I knew I needed to add a cheese element to the filling. Ricotta worked perfectly as it kept it as close as possible to my grandmother's recipe.

For the sugar syrup, put all the ingredients in a saucepan, bring to a boil and leave to simmer for 5 to 10 mins until it's slightly thickened. Put aside until needed.

Mix the nuts, brown sugar and cinnamon in a pan until it's all evenly coated and the sugar has melted on the nuts. Be careful to do this on a medium heat as the sugar can burn quickly. Set aside until you've baked the knafeh.

Shred the kataifi with your hands or scissors. This process takes the longest but it's worth it. Make sure to get roughly 2cm sized vermicelli-like strands of the pastry. Mix the melted butter and oil and pour it on the kataifi, making sure it's all evenly coated.

To make the filling, warm the single cream and mix in the cornflour and caster sugar to thicken it. Keep mixing until the cream really changes in consistency. In order to avoid getting lumps from the cornflour, dilute it in a little bit of milk before pouring it into the cream.

In a separate bowl, mix the ricotta cheese with the rose water. Once the cream has cooled slightly, combine it with the ricotta and you're ready to assemble.

Since you've coated your kataifi in lots of butter and oil, there is no need to line your baking tray with any additional butter. Use half of the pastry to fill the bottom of the dish then evenly spoon the filling on top, without touching the edges. Use the remaining kataifi to cover the filling. At this point, you can cover it and leave it overnight in the fridge if you do not plan to bake it and serve it straight away.

To bake it, preheat your oven to 180°C (fan) and bake it for 30-40 mins. Take it out when the pastry looks golden brown and crunchy. For a 33cm tray, it takes about 40 mins in the oven.

Pour 2/3 of the sugar syrup all over the knafeh as soon as you take it out of the oven. Listen to the sound it makes as the syrup touches the bottom of the tray! This makes it slightly less sweet than your typical shop bought knafeh. Leave the remaining sugar syrup on the table for people to add according to their preferences. Sprinkle the nuts all over the knafeh and tuck in.
Sahtein!

PASTRY & DOUGHS

Photography by @KatieWilsonFoto
Styling by @lily_vanilli_cake

SESAME - HALVA "1001 FEUILLES"

Donated by Myriam Sabet of Maison Aleph
@maisonaleph

"Food, music and languages are part of our emotional DNA. Celebrating Syrian gastronomic heritage while donating to such a great humanitarian cause is an honour to Maison Aleph. We are so thankful that initiatives like #CookForSyria and #BakeForSyria have been created."

Makes about 35 squares

For the filling

113g unsalted butter, at room temperature

120g halva (or vanilla halva)

75g tahini, stir before measuring

120g icing sugar

2 1/2 tbsp cornstarch

1/2 tsp fleur de sel (or 1/4 teaspoon fine sea salt)

3 large eggs, at room temperature

50g toasted white sesame seeds

For the layers

28 sheets filo dough (12-x-17 inches), thawed

360 ml clarified butter (from 454g butter)

around 180g confectioners' sugar

To garnish:

around 2 tbsp white sesame seeds

When I was a child growing up in Aleppo, my favorite afternoon snack was halva paste wrapped in a flat bread with butter. It was ecstatic and so addictive. I have always wanted to share that flavour and experience and introduce it to my fellow Parisians. Maison Aleph came up with a recipe around the three textures of sesame: paste, cream and seeds, making it completely addictive with clarified butter. I like to think of our Sesame-Halva "1001 Feuilles" as a free interpretation of baklava.

To make the filling: Working with a mixer fitted with a paddle attachment, beat the butter, halva and tahini on medium speed for about 3 mins. Add the confectioners' sugar, cornstarch and salt and mix on low for around 2 mins. One by one, add the eggs, beating for a minute after each goes in; you'll have a thick, smooth, shiny mixture. Stir in the sesame seeds. Scrape the filling into a bowl, cover and refrigerate for 1 hour (or for up to 2 days; the longer the better).

To build the layers: Lay the filo out on a piece of plastic wrap and cover with a damp kitchen towel. Always keep the towel moistened – the dough dries in a flash.

Brush the interior of a rimmed baking sheet (30cm x 45cm) with clarified butter. Place a sheet of dough in the pan, brush with butter and dust lightly with confectioners' sugar (use about 2 tbsp sugar per sheet). Continue until you've made 14 layers. Spread the filling evenly over the top and then continue making layers with the remaining dough. Butter and sugar the top layer (you'll have some butter leftover; hold on to it). Refrigerate the set-up for at least 30 mins (or cover and refrigerate for up to 1 day).

Center a rack in the oven and preheat it to 180°C. Using a pizza cutter (best) or sharp knife, trim the edges (don't remove them), then cut as many 2-inch squares as possible, cutting all the way through the layers. Scatter the sesame seeds over the top.

Bake for about 40 mins, rotating the pan after 20, until the top is beautifully golden. Transfer to a cooling rack and lightly brush with some of the reserved butter. Place a piece of parchment or foil over the surface, top with another baking pan and press evenly and firmly to compact the layers. Re-cut the squares, so they'll be easy to lift out. Let sit for 2 to 3 hours before serving (discard or nibble the trimmed edges). Stored tightly covered, the squares will keep at room temperature for about 2 days.

PASTRY & DOUGHS

Photography by @csmiskin
Portrait by Caspar Miskin

3. MINI CAKES & TRAY BAKES

—

TAHINI BROWNIES

Donated by Yotam Ottolenghi and Helen Goh
@ottolenghi @helen_goh_bakes

"As one of the greatest humanitarian crises of our time, the Syrian crisis is one that is impossible to ignore. We are privileged to have the opportunity, no matter how small, to do something to help."

Serves 12

250g unsalted butter, cut into 2cm cubes, plus extra for greasing

250g dark chocolate (70% cocoa solids), broken into 3-4cm pieces

4 large eggs

280g caster sugar

120g plain flour

30g dutch-processed cocoa powder

½ tsp salt

200g halva, broken into 2cm pieces

80g tahini paste

Like everyone else, we love a good brownie. The addition of tahini with its slight bitter note offsets the sweetness beautifully. The chunks of halva add textural interest and highlight the delicious sesame flavour. The combination is so good that some members of staff had to enforce a temporary ban on eating these particular brownies while creating the recipe. In order to achieve the perfect balance of cakey and gooey, the cooking time is crucial. It will vary by a minute or so between different ovens, and depending on where the tray is sitting in the oven, so keep a close eye on them.

Preheat the oven to 200°C/180°C Fan/Gas Mark 6. Grease and line a 23cm square or 30x20cm rectangular baking tin with baking parchment and set aside.

Place the butter and chocolate in a heatproof bowl over a pan of simmering water, making sure that the base of the bowl is not touching the water. Leave for about 2 mins, to melt, then remove from the heat. Stir through, until you have a thick shiny sauce. Set aside until room temperature.

Place the eggs and sugar in a large bowl and whisk until pale and creamy and a trail is left behind when you move the whisk. Add the chocolate and fold through gently using a spatula – don't over-work the mix here.

Sift the flour, cocoa and salt into a bowl, then gently fold into the chocolate mixture. Finally, add the pieces of halva, gently fold through the mix, then pour or scrape the mixture into the lined baking tin, using a small spatula to even it out. Dollop small spoonfuls of the tahini paste into the mix in about 12 different places, then use a skewer to swirl them through to create a marbled effect, taking the marbling right to the edges of the tin.

Bake for about 23 mins, until the middle has a slight wobble and it is gooey inside – they may be ready anywhere between 22 and 25 mins. If using the 30 x 20cm tin, they will need a couple of minutes less. They may seem a little undercooked at first, but they firm up once they start to cool down. If you want to serve them warm-ish (and gooey), set aside for just 30 mins before cutting into 16 pieces. Otherwise, set aside for longer to cool to room temperature.

These keep well for up to 5 days in an airtight container. They also freeze well, wrapped in cling film, for up to a month.

MINI CAKES AND TRAY BAKES

Photography by @pedenmunk
Portrait by @patricianiven

SPICED POMEGRANATE MOLASSES & PISTACHIO CAKE WITH ROSE WATER

Donated by Anna Hansen of the Modern Pantry
@themodernpantry

"I simply cannot fathom what it would be like to have my home, my family, my job or my life suddenly torn from me. It makes my heart ache to think about the pain and suffering the Syrian people are going through. I wanted to do something to help and this is what inspired this recipe. The flavours I have used reflect how I see the people of Syria and their strength, their warmth, their sheer determination and their bravery in the face of such adversity."

Serves 12

For the cake
150 g self raising flour

1 ½ tsp ground sumac

1 tsp ground cinnamon

1 tsp Aleppo chilli

½ tsp baking soda

150 g soft brown sugar

125 ml vegetable oil

2 large eggs

zest of 1 orange

135 g grated raw beetroot

100 g pomegranate molasses roast grapes, roughly chopped

60 g pistachios, toasted and roughly chopped

Pomegranate molasses roast grapes
400 g destalked and washed red seedless grapes

3 tbsp pomegranate molasses

2 tbsp rose water

1 ½ tbsp demerara sugar

Rose water drizzle icing
1 cup icing sugar, sifted

1 tbsp rose water

1 tbsp lemon juice

I am a massive fan of the bold, bright and warming flavours of Syria and the Middle East and incorporate them into my cooking almost every day. Here I use a few of my all time favourites: pomegranate molasses, rose water, Aleppo chilli and sumac. All of them are aromatic and robust and this super simple cake recipe is the perfect vehicle for showcasing them. Try using other root vegetables such as parsnips or carrots, or using figs instead of grapes and change up your spice combinations. Try different nuts or don't use them at all!

For the cake
Sift the flour, sumac, cinnamon and baking soda together. In another bowl whisk the sugar together with the vegetable oil, eggs, orange zest and Aleppo chilli. Stir in the grated beetroot, roast grapes and toasted pistachios then fold in the sifted dry ingredients.

Butter (or oil for a dairy free recipe) a 20cm cake tin and dust with demerara sugar, pour in the batter and bake for 20 mins. The cake is cooked when a wooden skewer inserted into the middle of the cake comes out clean.

Remove from the oven and place on a cake rack to cool. Turn the cake out of the tin after 15 mins and leave to cool completely. Ice with the rose water drizzle icing. Serve with a generous dollop of crème fraiche.

For the pomegranate molasses roast grapes
Put the grapes in a roasting tray just large enough to hold the grapes. Sprinkle over the sugar, pomegranate molasses and rose water and roast at 160°C for 15 to 20 mins. The grapes should just be starting to collapse in on themselves. Remove from the oven and leave to cool in their juices.

For the rose water drizzle icing
Mix the icing sugar, lemon juice and rose water together until lump free.

Photography by @chris.terry.photography

POMEGRANATE TEA CAKES DF

Donated by Lily Vanilli
@lily_vanilli_cake

"I'm grateful for the opportunity #CookForSyria and now #BakeForSyria has given me to do something to help those affected by a humanitarian crisis which has been heartbreaking to watch unfold while feeling powerless to help. Serena and Clerkenwell Boy came up with a way to turn a lot of people's good will into something that can actually help others, and the project not only raises significant money to help children affected by the war in Syria but endeavours to celebrate Syrian cuisine and culture and create joy."

Serves 15

For the cake

220g plain flour

200g caster sugar

1 tsp baking soda

1/2 tsp salt

240ml soy (or other non-dairy) milk

2 tsp black (or other) tea leaves

80ml olive oil

15ml white vinegar

For the icing

1 can coconut cream

50-100g icing sugar

To decorate

seeds from one large pomegranate

I have made these cakes with dried hibiscus before and you could do the same, just leave the hibiscus a little bit longer to infuse with the butter. Both black tea and zouhourat (made with hibiscus) are traditional Syrian teas and work well infused into a classically English cake. I know this isn't really a traditional English recipe but I wanted to make sure there was a dairy free option in the book. You could use any tea cake recipe you like and infuse butter rather than the oil in the same way.

Cake
Preheat oven to 180°C.

Heat the oil gently in a pan with the tea leaves for around 3 mins on a very low heat. Allow to cool and steep for a minimum of one hour then pass through a fine sieve to strain the leaves. (You could leave some leaves in for added flavour if you like, though they will continue to infuse throughout and after cooking so don't overdo it).

Combine the sugar, baking soda and salt evenly.

Combine the soy (non dairy) milk, infused olive oil and vinegar and whisk together with the dry ingredients until you have a nice smooth batter.

Divide the mixture into individual cake tins greased with a little more olive oil (I used mini brioche tins), filling ¾ of the way to the top.

Bake for 15 mins, or until a cocktail stick inserted into the centre comes out clean. Remove from the oven and leave to cool completely.

Once cool, pipe or dollop a dab of icing over the top and finish with pomegranate seeds.

Icing
Chill your coconut cream in the fridge overnight.

Remove the coconut cream from the fridge, don't tip or shake the tin as you want it to have separated in the can.

Scoop out just the thick cream at the top.

Place the hardened cream in a mixing bowl. Beat briefly with a mixer until just creamy.

Then add 50g of the sugar and mix until smooth – about a minute. You can always add a little more sugar to get the consistency you want – just add slowly and beat after each addition.

Photography by @KatieWilsonFoto
Styling by @lily_vanilli_cake
Portait by @alice_whitby

LITTLE DOUBLE CHOCOLATE TAHINI CAKES

Donated by Chloé Ride
@kloelladeville

"I've always believed that people need to stick together in tough circumstances, and our brothers and sisters in Syria need all our support right now. Since I've lived in Dubai, I've met many Syrian people who have left their country and moved here. My landlord is Syrian. The lady who works at the coffee shop I go to every morning is Syrian. It becomes real when you hear people talking about Aleppo as a place people used to go and discover on long weekends. Syrian people are some of the most loving, warm and family-oriented I've ever met and this project is an amazing way to make a positive change."

Makes 10-12 cakes

115g unsalted butter

130g plain flour

¾ tsp baking powder

150g caster sugar

2 free range eggs

150g 80% dark chocolate, melted

1 tsp vanilla extract

baking spray, for oiling

3 tbsp tahini

110g good quality white chocolate

1 tsp white sesame seeds, toasted

Tahini is commonly used throughout Middle Eastern cooking in both sweet and savoury dishes. Its salty, nutty undertones make it the perfect accompaniment to chocolate. These little cakes have a brownie-like texture on top, which crackles when you bite into them, followed by a light but intensely flavored sponge. Mixing white chocolate with tahini tempers its super sweet flavour and leaves you with a mouthful of perfectly balanced bliss!

Melt the butter and allow to cool slightly.

Mix the plain flour, baking powder, and salt in a medium bowl. Stir through the caster sugar. In a separate large bowl, whisk the eggs, vanilla and melted dark chocolate until the eggs are light and frothy, then stir through the flour mix until just combined. Pour in the melted butter and stir until everything is bought together.

Preheat the oven to 170°C.

Brush a 12 hole friand or small cake tin with a little melted butter and spoon the batter into each hole until it's ¾ full.

Bake the cakes for 12-15 mins or until the top is set.

Leave to cool slightly in the mould, then remove to cool completely on a wire rack.

Place the tahini and white chocolate in a glass bowl set over a saucepan of simmering water, making sure the bowl does not touch the water. Stir over a low heat until melted. Alternatively, place the bowl in the microwave and stir every thirty seconds until melted. Drizzle over the cakes and sprinkle with the toasted sesame seeds.

Photography by @murrindie
Styling by @kloelladeville

TAHINI AND SOUR CHERRY CUPCAKES

Donated by Jemma Wilson
@cupcakegemma

"Being involved in #BakeForSyria is such a thrill for me. I get to work alongside some of my baking heroes and raise money for an incredibly important cause, all while tickling your tastebuds, opening you up to the wonder of Syrian flavours and fuelling your passion for baking. It's nothing short of brilliant!"

For the cupcakes
135g unsalted butter, soft
50g tahini
125g caster sugar
125g self-raising flour
Pinch of salt
1/4 tsp bicarbonate of soda
2 large free-range eggs
1 1/2 tbsp milk

For the two buttercreams
150g unsalted butter, soft
340g icing sugar, sifted
1 tbsp milk
2 tbsp tahini
2 tbsp sour cherry syrup

To finish
12 Amarena cherries + their syrup
1 tbsp toasted sesame seeds

One of my favourite flavour combos of all time is peanut butter and jam and we bake a lot of kick-ass 'PB&J' cakes and cookies in the Crumbs & Doilies shop. I wanted to see if I could 'Syrianise' this classic combo and have come up with a belter! The Tahini and Sour Cherry Cupcake. I realise that 'T&SC' isn't quite as catchy but I promise that if you love 'PB&J' you're going to go crazy for this cupcake. Syrian sour cherries are not so easy to come by, but after some tests I found that Italian Amarena cherries are a brilliant alternative. They can be found in most Italian delis, so you should be able to get hold of some pretty easily.

Preheat your oven to 170°C and line a 12-hole cupcake tin with paper cases.

In a large bowl, put the butter, sugar, tahini, flour, salt, bicarb and eggs and beat together on a medium speed for 1 minute using an electric mixer or free-standing mixer. Give the bowl a scrape down to gather up any unmixed nuggets at the bottom of the bowl, add the milk and beat for another minute.

Scoop an equal amount into your 12 cupcake cases then bake for 19-21 mins until springy to the touch. Leave to cool.

To make the buttercream, in a clean bowl beat the soft butter for around 5 mins on a high speed until much paler in colour and light and whippy.

Add the sifted icing sugar in two halves, beating for 2-3 mins after each addition. Divide as evenly as possible into two bowls. Into one, add the milk and tahini and beat for a couple of mins, adding more liquid if you need to. In the other bowl add the syrup from the cherry jar and do the same. Both buttercreams should be silky and spreadable.

To finish off your cupcakes, place a large star nozzle into a piping bag and, lying it flat on the counter, build up a layer of each flavour inside the piping bag, being careful not to mix the two together too much.

Pipe a generous swirl of the two-flavour buttercream on top of each cupcake.

To finish, pop a single sour cherry on top with a drizzle of the syrup and sprinkle with the toasted sesame seeds.

Photography by @KatieWilsonFoto
Styling by @clerkenwellboyec1

PISTACHIO TRES LECHES CAKE

Donated by David Muniz and David Lesniak of Outsider Tart
@outsidertart

"For us, being American means growing up with all sorts of global influences in the kitchen. Food has a way of bringing people together and this is what we love about what we do. The best experiences for us are often helping people when they are at their worst. It's only then that you realize the power of ingredients, and just how much relief or joy they can bring when combined just so. It is the simplest of gestures with the greatest reward."

For the batter

Approx. 225g roasted pistachios, preferably unsalted

450g all-purpose or plain flour

1 tbsp plus 1 tsp baking powder

¾ tsp (omit if nuts are salted) kosher salt

225g unsalted butter

450g granulated Sugar

4 large eggs

240ml whole milk

For the milk syrup

360ml whole milk

120ml condensed milk

360ml evaporated milk

2 tsp orange zest, grated (if using orange blossom water)

60ml rose or orange blossom water

For the whipped cream

460ml heavy or double cream

4 tbsp confectioners or icing sugar

1 tbsp or to taste rose or orange blossom water

For this recipe we adapted the Cuban family favourite Tres Leches Cake, to create a Pistachio and Rose version. We added ground nuts and replaced the vanilla, rum and lime from the original with rose water and pistachios. It is a sweet, gooey confection, very informal, inviting and sure to lift anyone's spirits.

Preheat the oven to 180°C.
Butter a 23 x 23 x 5 cm pan, line the bottom and two sides with parchment, making sure to leave an extra 1.5cm of parchment on either side. Dust the remaining two side lightly with flour.

Finely grind the nuts, setting aside 115g.

Whisk together the remaining nuts, flour, baking powder and salt. Set aside.

Beat butter and sugar until light and fluffy. Reduce the speed to medium and add the eggs, beating to combine well. Scrape the bowl and mix for 1 minute more until everything is light, fluffy and smooth. On low speed alternately add the flour and milk. Begin and end with the dry ingredients and mix only until just combined. Pour the batter into the prepared pan and smooth with a spatula.

Bake for 30 to 35 mins or until a toothpick emerges clean from the center. Cool cake in the pan.

Combine the three milks and zest (if using) in a saucepan over medium heat. Stirring often, heat until it is smooth and steaming. Not boiling.

Pierce the cake all over. Slowly pour the warm milk syrup over it gradually. Cool completely then refrigerate overnight.

For the whipped cream

Whisk together cream, sugar and rose water on low speed. As the volume of the cream begins to increase, slowly increase to medium. Continue whisking until you have soft peaks, up to 10 mins.

To finish the cake, remove the bowl from the mixer and finish whisking by hand until the cream firms up slightly more. It never takes long and it's the best way to avoid over whisking. It should be luxuriously thick and smooth but not at all grainy.

Carefully remove the chilled cake from the pan by grabbing the parchment on the sides and slowly lifting it, placing the whole lot on a serving platter. Ease the parchment out from underneath the cake. Spread the sweetened whipped cream liberally on the top. Finish with the remaining ground nuts.

MINI CAKES AND TRAY BAKES

Photography by @CharlotteHuCo
Styling by @lily_vanilli_cake

HALVA CANELÉ

Donated by Philippe Moulin of Babelle
@babelle_uk

"The reason for being involved in #CookForSyria / #BakeForSyria can be expressed through an excerpt from the song "We are the world": "We are the world We are the children We are the ones who make a brighter day, so let's start giving..." Everyone has to be empathetic and attentive to other people's problems. It is important to always try to be an agent of positive change, bringing joy and comfort to those who need it most."

Makes 16 canelés

500ml whole milk

100g unsalted butter, softened, plus extra to grease (optional)

½ vanilla pod, split

250g caster sugar

2 medium free-range eggs, plus 2 yolks

100g plain flour

8 x 70ml silicone canelé mould (We only use silicone moulds from the French brand "De Buyer")

For the ganache

360g of heavy cream

160g white chocolate

100g of halawa paste

A canelé is a traditional sweet delicacy from the Bordeaux region of France. The perfect canelé has to have a crisp, shiny golden brown exterior and a soft and custardy heart. This is a great recipe because it allows everyone (assuming that they follow the method carefully) to get a consistent result, so the canelés will always have the same delicious taste, the same beautiful color and the same unique texture. We have adapted the traditional canelé here with a Syrian twist.

For the canelés
Put the milk, butter and vanilla pod in a medium pan. Bring to a simmer, then remove from the heat and cool slightly. In a mixing bowl, whisk the sugar, eggs and egg yolks with a balloon whisk until pale and creamy, then whisk in the flour until smooth.

Discard the vanilla pod, then pour in a third of the milk mixture. Whisk to combine. Pour in the remaining mixture, stirring with the whisk, until combined into a pancake batter-like consistency. Chill the canelé mixture in the fridge for about 12 hours.

Butter the canelé moulds with plenty of butter, making sure the flutes are well greased. Heat the oven to 250°C/230°C fan/gas and put a baking sheet on the middle rack to heat up.
Stir the chilled mixture, then pour into the moulds to just below the rim. Bake on the sheet in the middle of the oven for 5 mins, then turn the oven down to 180Cª/160ªC fan/gas and bake for 60 mins more.
Leave the canelés to cool completely (for at least an hour) before turning out of the moulds. The're now ready to eat.

For the ganache
Boil the cream, then place chocolate and halva in a bowl. When the cream is fully boiling pour it over the chocolate and halva mix and let sit for a minute. Whisk all ingredients together, then let the ganache cool over an ice bath. Set for 4 hours in the fridge.

Now whip it up again by hand or with a mixer to thicken it. Rest again in the fridge to set. Soften enough (at room temp, or carefully heating it) to get it to a consistency you can pipe into your canelés - enjoy!

Photography by @CharlotteHuCo
Styling by @lily_vanilli_cake

BAKED CHEESECAKE, CANDIED BLOOD ORANGE & SWEET PISTACHIO DUKKAH GF

Donated by Tom Hill from Rawduck
@raw_duck

"The devastation in Syria is on such an enormous scale and the end doesn't seem to be in sight. It's hard to know what to do from here and it's easy to feel helpless. If there is anything we can do in our daily lives to raise awareness and make a positive difference, then that is a good start. I hope #BakeForSyria can bring support and some relief to people whose lives have been devastated by the conflict."

Makes 6 individual cakes

For the cheesecake
340g cream cheese
165ml double cream
120g unrefined golden caster sugar
20g gluten-free self raising flour
2 whole eggs

For the dukka (makes a little more than you need but will keep for a week or so)
125g shelled pistachios
50g unrefined caster sugar
25g toasted sesame seeds
zest of 1 orange
1tsp ground ginger
1/2 tsp ground cinnamon
1/2tsp garam masala
A pinch of Cornish sea salt

For the candied blood orange peel
2 blood oranges peeled
50g unrefined caster sugar
100ml water

We've chosen this recipe because it combines many loves in one recipe, taking its inspiration from Italy as well as the Middle East. The ricotta baked cheesecake is topped with candied orange, which is a speciality at a particular sweet shop in Trapani in Sicily. The sweet pistachio dukkah is inspired by the many Middle Eastern breakfasts we've enjoyed that consisted of dukkah or tatar, olive oil and flat bread.

For the cheesecake
Beat everything together in a food mixer until smooth.

Preheat the oven to 210°C.

Grease six 10cmx3cm cake tins then cut out a circle of greaseproof paper and roughly line, it doesn't need to be perfect as the folds add texture to the outside of the cheesecake, but tuck into the corners.

Fill each tin to almost the top of the tin, it will rise during cooking but will sink as it cools down.

Bake for 20-25 mins or until it is slightly coloured round the side but still has a little wobble in the middle.
Allow to cool then its best refrigerated overnight.

For the dukkah
Warm the pistachios in the oven but don't toast too much and then lightly crush.

Lightly toast the sesame seeds in a pan.
Then mix all the ingredients together.

For the candied blood orange peel
Slice the blood oranges into strips and then put into a small saucepan with the sugar and water.

Gently warm together to dissolve the sugar then simmer for 15 mins until the peel is soft, then turn up the heat and gently boil till most of the water has evaporated so it looks like a loose marmalade.

Allow to cool.

To serve
Take a large spoon and scoop out a portion of the cheesecake, scatter over the candied blood orange and then sprinkle over the dukka.

Photography by @KatieWilsonFoto
Styling by @lily_vanilli_cake
Plates by @kanalondon

4. COOKIES & GRAINS

—

DATE STUFFED MA'AMOUL

Donated by Ammar Awtani

500g plain flour
250g ghee
200ml water
200g sugar
10g yeast
500g medjool dates, stones removed.

Here is Ammar's recipe for ma'amoul, which he says is one of the oldest Syrian dishes you can find and famous from ancient times. Ammar describes the dish: "When a piece of Maamoul melts in your mouth, it takes you on a journey to a paradise for the senses. It is also a good source of various vitamins and minerals. It's a great start to the day!"

To make the filling
Process the dates in a food processor until smooth and set aside.

To make the dough
In a large bowl, mix the yeast with the flour.

Make a sugar syrup by boiling the water then adding the sugar and keep it at a rolling boil for one minute. Let cool slightly.

Melt the ghee, then add it slowly into the flour mixture, then add the sugar syrup and mix together into a dough. It will look quite sticky and wet but it will come together! Don't be tempted to add a lot more flour.

Pop the dough in the fridge to rest for about 30 mins, or 10 mins in the freezer.

To make the cookies
Preheat the oven to 200°C/190 fan.
Line two baking trays with baking parchment.
Divide the dough into 32 equal balls and do the same with the date paste (if it's very sticky, put a little vegetable oil on your hands first).

Take each ball of dough and roll it out into a disc, then place in the palm of your hand and put the date filling in the middle, then gently fold the edges together until it's all sealed. Pinch the join to make sure and placing that side underneath, flatten the ma'amoul slightly. You can score the top gently with a fork to make a pattern.

When you've filled all of them, place on the baking tray about 5cm apart and bake for around 15 mins until they're pale golden brown – don't let them get too dark.

Cool on a wire rack and dust with icing sugar.

They will keep for two weeks in an airtight container.

COOKIES & GRAINS

Photography by @KatieWilsonFoto
Styling by @lily_vanilli_cake

CHOCOLATE, SEA SALT AND TAHINI COOKIES

Donated by Leah Hyslop
@leah.hyslop

"I have always loved food's ability to connect people. It happens every day on a small scale, when you make dinner for a loved one or offer a friend in need a cup of tea. Magically, it can also create big projects like #CookForSyria – a supper club that has grown into a movement, raising awareness and funds for the Syrian crisis."

Makes 15-20 large cookies

160g plain flour

40g cocoa powder

1 scant tsp bicarbonate of soda

1 heaped tsp flaked sea salt, plus extra to serve

150g unsalted butter

125 caster sugar

90g dark soft brown sugar

100g tahini

1 large egg, beaten

80g dark chocolate, chopped roughly into chunks

A paste made from sesame seeds, Tahini is a cornerstone of Middle Eastern cuisine. In Syria, it's usually used in savoury dishes but it also works brilliantly in sweet treats, balancing out the sugar with a deep, rounded nuttiness. I like think of it as doing the same job as peanut butter in a PB&J sandwich. Here, I've used it to give a Syrian twist to classic chocolate cookies, with a little sea salt for extra grown-up oomph.

Preheat the oven to 180°C.

Line two large baking sheets with baking paper.

In a large bowl or stand mixer, cream the butter, sugars and tahini until creamy. Add the egg and mix well.

Using a sieve, sift the flour, cocoa and bicarbonate of soda into the bowl and mix gently to form a dough. Stir in the chocolate chunks and the sea salt.

Roll the dough into balls – I like mine slightly larger than a golf ball – and place, evenly spaced, on the lined trays. Bake for 12-15 mins.

Leave on the tray for 10 mins or so to set, then transfer to a cooling rack. Sprinkle with a little extra salt.

Photography by @CharlotteHuCo
Styling by @lily_vanilli_cake
Portrait by @nassimarothacker

SWEET FENNEL AND ROSE DUKKAH GF, DF

Donated by Sarah Lemanski of Noisette Bakehouse
@noisettebakehouse

"The ethos of cooking, sharing and nourishing with generosity and love is ingrained in the culture of Middle Eastern countries. This sentiment is universal, ultimately creating comfort and doing what all good food should do: bringing people together. It is great that this initiative can support that ethos while bringing help to Syrians affected by the conflict."

75g coconut flakes, toasted

1 tbsp rose water

4 tbsp whole almonds, skin on, toasted

1.5 tsp fennel seeds, toasted and ground

60g sesame seeds, toasted

60g desiccated coconut, untoasted

4 tbsp pistachio flakes, untoasted

3/4 tsp vanilla powder

1 tsp fresh ground mahlab*

1/2 tsp sea salt

8g dried edible rose petals

1 tbsp bee pollen (optional, omit if making this vegan)

*It is worthwhile searching for whole mahlab seeds online, they are sometimes a little harder to seek out than ground mahlab but the flavour of them is so much better.

Don't be put off by the list of ingredients here. It really is a simple recipe that offers huge rewards and will add bursts of flavour to a whole range of dishes, from morning porridge to late night ice cream bowls. My sweet dukkah was inspired by the versatility of the traditional dukkah spice blend. I craved a condiment with the same versatility, a combination of sweet spices, toasted nuts and seeds. The key to this recipe is capturing the perfect point of toasting!

Preheat the oven to 180°C and allow to heat up ready for the almond whilst you toast the coconut flakes.

Place the coconut flakes in a single layer in a non stick pan, for even toasting. Add the rose water and put the pan over a medium/low heat. The coconut will absorb the rose water and each chip will toast to a golden brown. Shuffle the chips around periodically to ensure even toasting. Remove from the pan and place in a bowl.

Now use the same pan to toast the sesame seeds, again ensuring they sit in an even layer in the pan and shake gently from time to time as they toast so they do not catch. You will most likely hear them start to gently pop. Remove from the heat and place in the bowl with the toasted coconut flakes.

Next place the whole almonds on a lined baking tray and toast at 180°C for 5 mins. Shuffle the nuts, then return to the oven for a further 5-7 mins. The skins should be darker in colour, with small blisters beginning to appear and the centres should be golden brown. When ready, remove and add to a small bowl to cool before chopping.

Finally place the fennel seeds in your pan and heat until intensely aromatic. You should be able to smell the anise and the seeds will have swelled slightly. Once toasted, place them in a pestle and mortar and grind to a medium fine dust.
Roughly chop the cooled almonds, with some chopped quite fine and others left chunky to allow for crunch and texture.

Combine everything evenly with your remaining ingredients.

Pour into a clean airtight jar where it will be at its best for up to 2 months

Photography by @noisettebakehouse
Portrait by @helenadolby

MA'AMOUL RECIPE

Donated by John Gregory-Smith
@johngs

"Millions of displaced Syrians need our help urgently. They need food and safe shelter, and above all, happiness once again. This is a great start. Getting involved and having people buy the book raises much needed cash that goes directly to the people who need it."

For the biscuits

250g butter

a small pinch of saffron

500g fine semolina

55g plain flour

100g caster sugar

1 tsp baking powder

2 tbsp rose water

60 ml whole milk

salt

For the filling

600g medjool dates

2 tbsp rose water

3 tsp cinnamon

These decadent date biscuits are a Syrian staple. They are such a classic Middle Eastern biscuit that every mum will make them. Traditionally ma'amoul are made using an eccentric wooden mould that shapes the biscuits into wonderful geometric patterns. You push the dough into the oiled mould and then bash it against a board to get the biscuits back out. If you don't own one, you can shape the ma'amoul by hand. I have made my ma'amoul with saffron infused butter to give another level of fragrance and added rose water and cinnamon to the dates.

Melt the butter over a low heat. Add the saffron. Remove from the heat and leave to infuse, stirring occasionally, for 5 mins.

Combine semolina and butter in a bowl. Take a handful of the semolina and rub it between your hands over a shallow dish. This separates out the grains and helps them swell up. Repeat until all the semolina is done. Cover and leave for one hour or overnight in the fridge.

Add the flour, sugar, baking powder and a pinch of salt to the semolina. Rub it all together with your hands. Add the rose water and milk, and bring together into a dough. Work into a ball and place in a bowl. Cover and set aside to rest for one hour. Divide into 32 portions and roll each one into a ball.

Filling

Blitz dates with rose water and cinnamon in a food processor to a coarse, sticky paste. Wet your hands and roll the date paste into 32 small balls.

Pre-heat oven to 180 fan. Take one of the dough portions and, holding it in the palm of your hand, press your thumb into the centre. Work your thumb around opening the dough up into a cup shape that is big enough to hold one of the date balls inside. Place date ball in the centre and close the pastry back over the top. Roll into a ball. Repeat.

If using a ma'amoul mould, oil it and make your ma'amoul by pushing a finished date-dough ball into the mould, and knocking it back out. If not, flatten each ma'amoul into a small round biscuit, about 2 inches wide and about ¾ cm thick. Place onto a lined baking tray. Bake for 12-15 mins until the side of the biscuits have gone golden. Remove from the oven and leave to cool completely. Serve immediately.

Photography by @CharlotteHuCo
Styling by @lily_vanilli_cake
Portrait by @alan.keohane

GRAYBEH COOKIE

Donated by Dalia Dogmoch Soubra
@daliaskitchen

"My family is Syrian, but I grew up in Europe. We used to visit family in Syria every year before the war broke out, which has now displaced my family and also kept me away from Syria since 2011. Keeping Syrian recipes alive has become a personal wish of mine, and this initiative strikes a very personal note for my entire family and me."

Makes approx. 60 Cookies

110g icing sugar, sifted

180ml clarified butter (may substitute with soft butter)

1 tsp orange blossom

½ tsp salt

¼ tsp ground cardamom

200g flour, sifted

100g almond flour

50g pistachio flour (may substitute with additional almond meal)

shelled pistachios to garnish

Ghraybeh must be every Syrian's favourite cookie. I have countless memories of eating a tin full of these buttery, crumbly cookies at my grandmother's house in Damascus. They are so simple yet so distinctly Syrian in flavour. The hint of pistachio and butter and that subtle touch of orange blossom add a special Middle Eastern touch to the cookies. Ghraybeh and Barazek (recipe is in the #CookForSyria book) are favourite traditional Syrian cookies.

Using an electric mixer or hand whisk, cream the sugar, butter, orange blossom, salt and cardamom together.

Add the flour, almond and pistachio flour, and mix well.

Using your hands, make 2cm round balls and place them on a tray lined with parchment paper.

Gently press one pistachio onto the top of each cookie.

Place the cookies in the fridge for at least 30 mins.

In a 160°C-preheated oven, bake the Ghraybeh cookies for about 12-14 mins, making sure not to brown them. Ideally the cookies should be cooked through but remain white in colour.

Let the cookies cool and store in an airtight container.

SYRIAN BISCUIT BIRDS

Donated by Frances Quinn
@frances_quinn

"I am so proud to be part of the #BakeForSyria campaign and help raise awareness and funds for such a great cause. I loved creating my bespoke Syrian Bird Biscuits and hope that this recipe together with all the other incredible contributions will help ensure that the #BakeForSyria book flies off the shelf."

Biscuit Dough
150g butter, softened
150g caster sugar
1 egg
1 tbsp vanilla extract
300g plain flour

Decoration
runny honey
shelled pistachios
dried rose petals

These biscuit birds have become something of a signature bake of mine, so I couldn't think of a better recipe to give a Syrian twist for this book. I have used my basic vanilla butter biscuit dough, but adapted it with ingredients and flavours associated with Syrian cuisine. The honey acts like a glue to attach the pistachio slices and dried rose petals to the biscuits, creating a textured plumage and flavoursome collection of feathers.

Beat together the butter and sugar for 3–5 mins or until smooth and creamy.

Beat the egg with the vanilla extract in a mug with a fork. Gradually add to the creamed mixture, beating well. Sift the flour into the mixture in two or three batches, mixing gently, to make a soft dough.

Halve the dough and wrap in clingfilm. Refrigerate for several hours, preferably overnight, to firm up. You'll only need one of the pieces of dough for this recipe. Keep the second one in the fridge and use within a week, or freeze it.

Remove the piece of dough from the fridge 15–30 mins before rolling, so it can soften slightly. Halve the piece of dough. Take one half and roll it out on baking paper to the thickness of a £1 coin. If the dough seems very sticky, lightly dust it and the parchment with a little flour.

Using a bird shaped cutter, cut out your shapes from the dough. Peel away the excess dough and slide your bird lined parchment on to a flat baking tray and refrigerate for 15 mins. Re-roll the trimmings to cut out more birds on another piece of parchment the same as before.

Preheat the oven to 180°C/160°C fan/gas 4 while the biscuits are chilling.

Remove the bird lined baking trays from the fridge and before baking use the end of a cocktail stick to create the indent of an eye on the birds.

Bake for about 10-15 mins or until lightly golden brown around the edges.

Leave to firm up on the tray for a few mins before transferring, on the parchment, to a wire rack to cool.

To decorate the bird biscuits, take your pistachios and carefully slice into fine slithers. Then using the runny honey and a paintbrush, apply a thin coating of honey like glue onto the bird biscuits. Sprinkle and press the pistachio slices and rose petals over to create a feather effect.

SYRIAN FLORENTINES

Donated by Jennifer Earle
@jennifer.earle

"I feel incredibly privileged while also generally feeling so powerless to bring about change for people who are suffering. The #CookForSyria project is inspiring. It has so many wonderful and influential people involved and it really feels like change is possible and people are being helped. I want to do anything I can to help it grow."

Makes about 12 biscuits

40 butter

50g white sugar

20g pomegranate molasses

80g chopped walnuts and pistachios, whole pinenuts (these are optional and I wouldn't use more than 10g) plus sesame seeds

25g plain flour

150g dark chocolate

Typically florentines are made with a combination of nuts and dried fruits, but I have used pomegranate molasses for a Syrian twist. It provides the same fruity notes while keeping the texture all about the nuts. If you especially want dried fruit then sour cherries are delicious in the mix and appropriately Syrian.

Preheat oven to 160C (fan).

Line a baking tray with greaseproof paper.
Weigh the nuts and then chop the walnuts and pistachios into smaller pieces.

Heat the butter and sugar into saucepan until just the butter is melted. Remove from heat.

Stir the nuts and seeds with 20g flour in a small bowl.

Stir 20g pomegranate molasses into the sugar and butter.
Tip the dry ingredients into the saucepan and stir.

Use your hands to form small balls of the mixture (about the size of a walnut). Place on the tray with very large gaps in between to allow for spreading and flatten them a little into circles.

Place the tray in the oven for 9-12 mins, until fully spread and golden brown.

Remove from the oven and use a spoon or knife to push the biscuits into neater circles. Leave to cool completely.

Once the biscuits are cool weigh out 100g of chopped chocolate into a microwave-safe bowl.

Heat for a minute on a medium-high setting. Stir and return to the microwave for 30 second bursts until all the chocolate is melted.
Add 40g of the remaining chocolate. Stir until all of the lumps of chocolate are removed. Leave for 30 seconds and prepare a cooling rack.

Use a spoon to spread the chocolate on the biscuits and sit them chocolate-side up on the cooling rack. As the chocolate cools, drag a fork across it to create patterns in the chocolate. You'll need to stop to do this after every 3-4 biscuits are coated with chocolate as the chocolate should set quickly.

COOKIES & GRAINS

Photography by @CharlotteHuCo
Styling by @lily_vanilli_cake

TAHINI TOFFEE COOKIES

Donated by Rachel Khoo
@rachelkhooks

"My editorial team Khoollect and I got involved in #CookForSyria with a spiced semolina apple cake and so it felt only natural to get involved with #BakeForSyria too. It's wonderful to see how this worthy cause has been supported by so many foodies across the world."

Serves 12-16

115g soft unsalted butter
80g soft brown sugar
80g caster sugar
120g tahini well stirred
2 medium eggs
1 tsp vanilla extract
75g plain flour
75g whole-wheat flour
1 tsp sea salt plus a little extra
100g walnuts roughly chopped
200g chewy chocolate toffees

It's hard to beat a chewy dense cookie but using tahini takes this cookie to another level. The tahini lends a nuttier note but also a saltiness which works well with toffee. I've used brown sugar to give the cookies more of a caramel kick and whole-wheat flour for a more rustic flavour. The dough is especially moreish and even I find it hard to resist (I'm not usually one to eat cookie dough!) Try to use harder chewy toffees rather than softer ones, as they tend to simply melt into the dough when baked (although there's nothing wrong with that).

Preheat oven to 160°C fan.

Beat the sugar, butter, tahini and vanilla essence until just creamed together (don't over-beat). Add the eggs and continue to beat until combined. Mix together the flours and salt. Fold into the mix with the toffees until the flour is incorporated.

Use an ice-cream scoop to portion out cookies on to a baking tray lined with baking paper. Leave plenty of space between the cookies as they spread a lot.

Bake for 12-15 mins. Sprinkle with a little more sea salt if desired and leave to cool on a rack.

Photography by @CharlotteHuCo
Styling by @lily_vanilli_cake

SYRIAN GRANOLA DF

Donated by Dana Elemara of Arganic
@arganic

"As an Iraqi hearing stories first-hand of people left helpless by war, the crisis in Syria is all too familiar and breaks my heart. Syria is known to have some of the best cuisine in the Middle East and #CookForSyria is a brilliant initiative that at the very least shows that so many of us care."

Serves 6

2 cups of oats

1 cup walnuts roughly chopped

⅓ cup of pistachios

3 tbsp of sesame seeds

1 flat tsp of fennel seeds

½ tsp ground cardamom or seeds from 3 whole pods crushed

½ tsp cinnamon

generous pinch of salt

4 tbsp of olive or argan oil

2 tbsp of honey

6 medjool dates

zest of 1 orange

This is a nice and fragrant Syrian-inspired granola using typical Arabic store cupboard ingredients. It's quick to make and works well as a gift. I always make fragrant granolas like this and though it's usually impromptu, I end up using these staple Arabic ingredients. The orange zest, fennel seeds and cardamom really give this granola an edge. It's definitely worth using flavoursome medjool over regular dates in this recipe.

Preheat oven to 160°C, and line a baking tray with greaseproof paper.

In a large bowl, add all the dry ingredients including the orange zest but not the dates, and mix well. Then stir in the oil and honey so that everything is coated. Spread the mixture onto the lined baking tray so that you get a thin layer.

Bake for 25 mins, stirring the mixture halfway through.

Pit and chop the dates and add into the mixture at the end, while it's still warm out of the oven. Leave to cool then store in an airtight container. I recommend enjoying this with full fat yoghurt drizzled with a very good quality oil (either a peppery olive oil or a nutty oil) and honey or date syrup, with a side of refreshing fruit.

Photography by @KatieWilsonFoto
Styling by @lily_vanilli_cake

ZA'ATAR AND SHANKLISH SCONES WITH SMOKED LABNEH

Donated by Ravinder Bhogal of Jikoni
@cookinboots

"I think the #CookForSyria campaign is hugely inspiring because it has been led by a small group of energetic and passionate people who have helped shine light on one of the world's worst humanitarian crises through something as accessible as food. If my culinary skills can make even a jot of difference or support this amazing campaign then I am all for it."

225g spelt flour

75g shankleesh cheese, finely crumbled

10 black or green olives, pitted and chopped

1 tbsp za'atar

½ tsp paprika

1 egg

2 tbsp milk

1.5 tbsp baking powder

3 tbsp extra virgin olive oil

¼ tsp sea salt

black pepper to taste

For garnishing

1 tbsp milk

1 tbsp za'atar

For the smoked labneh

500g full fat yoghurt

sea salt and freshly ground black pepper

¼ tsp of crushed garlic

I love afternoon tea, but it's the savoury stuff that really lights my fire. Za'atar is a heady spice mix made with salt, sumac, thyme and sesame seeds and once you've eaten it you'll be reaching for it as often as salt and pepper. These savoury scones are irresistible and will make you forget about any hankerings for jam and clotted cream. They are pumped full of good things like olives and shanklish and the smoked labneh elevates them to a whole other level. If you can't find shanklish, feta or soft goats cheese are great substitutes.

For the smoked labneh, mix the yoghurt with salt, pepper and garlic. Line a sieve with a layer of muslin, making sure it hangs over the edges. Pour in your yoghurt, gather up the ends of the cloth and tie them up. Hang in the fridge over a bowl to drain for at least 4 hours or preferably overnight.

When you are ready to smoke, light a piece of coal until smoldering and ashen. Using a pair of tongs put it into a small heatproof bowl. Put the labneh into a large bowl. Place the small bowl of coal on top of the yoghurt. Pour a teaspoon of oil on the coal – it will begin to smoke immediately - cover the large bowl tightly to contain all the smoke and leave for half an hour.

Make the scones
Preheat the oven to 220°C.

Sift the flour and baking powder into a bowl. Add salt, paprika and olive oil and lightly mix with the tips of your fingers until you have a coarse crumb like texture. Now sprinkle in the za'atar, feta and olives, and mix.

In a separate bowl, beat together the egg and the milk. Pour into the flour a little at a time, kneading lightly until you have dough that is soft but not sticky.

Lightly dust a surface with flour. Roll out the dough to a 2 inch thickness and stamp out circles of the dough using a 2 inch cutter. Place the scones on a lined baking sheet and brush with milk and sprinkle with more za'atar. Bake for 12 - 15 mins, until golden and risen. Serve warm with smoked labneh

5. SAVOURY

—

THREE CHEESE ZA'ATAR ROLLS

Donated by James Thompson & Nigel Slater
@sloefilms @nigelslater

"We were lucky enough to visit the Middle East several times last year, filming a documentary for the BBC. In Beirut, we met a man whose ice-cream shop stayed open for all but two days of the 15-year civil war, closing only when shelling reached its doorstep. We asked the owner why he would put his life in such peril for the sake of ice cream: "In the face of such adversity, it is the little things like a favourite treat that can keep spirits up just enough to get you through the day"

Serves 8-10

375g all butter puff pastry
Plain flour for dusting
50g kashkaval cheese
125g mozzarella cheese
200g feta cheese
5 tbsp za'atar
1 egg, beaten
3 tbsp sesame seeds

Set the oven to 200°C.

Lightly flour a pastry board or work surface, then roll out the puff pastry in a rectangle about 35cm x 25cm.

Grate the kashkaval and mozzarella cheeses into a large bowl, crumble in the feta and add the za'atar. Mix the cheeses well using your hands.

Spread the cheese and za'atar mix over the pastry, leaving a small border around the edges of about 2cm. Brush one of the short ends with a little beaten egg.

Starting from the short un-brushed end, roll the pastry up into a cylinder sealing the join with more beaten egg. Fear not, the filling is deliberately generous. Tidiness isn't a priority here.

Cut into 8 or so 4cm thick slices. Place these flat on a baking sheet covered with baking parchment. Brush the sides with more egg, but not the top and then scatter a generous pinch of sesame seeds on each pastry.

Bake for 20 mins, till puffed and golden.

Photography by Jonathan Lovekin

LAHAM BAHINE

Donated by Pizza Pilgrims
@pizzapilgrims

"I found that the food is AMAZING in Syria! Beautifully spiced and bizarrely using a lot of the same ingredients as Italy"

Serves 4-5

For the dough
1kg high-gluten 00 flour
2g fresh baker's yeast
700ml cold water
30g table salt

For the topping
1 medium onion
500g ground beef, diced
70g tomato puree
mozzarella
basil
chicken stock
natural yoghurt
½ tsp cumin
½ tsp turmeric
1 tsp coriander
¼ tsp allspice
¼ tsp cinnamon
¼ tsp black pepper salt
pinch of za'atar spice mix to taste

The flatbreads from the Middle East are some of the best in the world and Syria actually has its own style of pizza called Laham Bajine. Our version is inspired by this, and also a little by manoushe breads from Lebanon. The only changes we've made are using our Neapolitan pizza dough and the addition of mozzarella. The za'atar spice mix is very common in Syrian cuisine.

To make the dough
Tip the flour on to your work surface and make a well in the centre. Dissolve the yeast in the water and pour into the middle of the well a little at a time, while using your hands to bring the walls of the flour in so that the water begins to thicken.

Once you've reached the consistency of custard, add the salt and bring in the rest of the flour until it comes together as a dough. Knead for 10-15 mins until firm. Cover and leave to rest for 10 mins before kneading again quickly for 10 seconds. (This helps to develop the flavour and the gluten.)

Divide the dough into 200g balls and leave to rest overnight, or for at least 8 hours (24 hours is optimal, 48 hours is the maximum) in a sealed container or a deep baking dish sprinkled with flour and covered in clingfilm. Remember to leave space for each of your dough balls because, as the gluten relaxes, they will spread out to take up twice the diameter that they do initially.

For the topping, brown off the beef mince in a heavy-bottomed pan in a tablespoon of olive oil. Add the onion and continue to fry off for 5-10 mins until the onions have softened. Add all the spices and cook through for 2-3 mins. Stir in the tomato purée and pour over the chicken stock. Simmer on a low heat for 45-60 mins with the lid on until the meat has softened and the sauce has reduced. (You may have to add water from time to time to stop it from drying out.)

Turn off the heat and leave to cool. Spread a good spoonful of the mixture onto your pizza base and top with mozzarella and basil. Bake in the hottest oven you can find, or use our frying pan technique on our website. Finish with natural yoghurt and a good pinch of the za'atar spice mix.

Photography by @joe_woodhouse

FATAYER BIL LAHME (MEAT PIES)

Donated by Mohammed Harrah

Makes 60 pies

For the filling

1kg fine mince meat

300g finely diced onion

1 tsp baharat spice (a blend of 7 spices found in Middle Eastern stores)

1 tsp salt

200ml pomegranate molasses

For the dough

100g butter, melted

1 full tsp fast-acting dry yeast

400-500ml lukewarm water

1kg flour

I am Mohamed from Aleppo. I lived there with my wife and nine children for my whole life. I have lots of grandchildren.

I have been a baker for most of my adult life, over 40 years. I had three shops in Aleppo – one sold meat pies and the other two shops sold sweet pastries. I am proud of the shops and business I ran. I belonged to the Guild of Bakers.

I lost my eyesight during a bombing in my town, which also destroyed one of my businesses. It became very unsafe for my wife, me and my youngest son, so we went to Turkey in the hope of medical care.

In 2015 I was given a chance to be resettled in the UK. We took this opportunity and came to Colchester in December 2015. I have done a bit of baking since arriving here.

Heat the oil in a frying pan over a medium-high heat and saute the onion until soft and fragrant. Add the meat, baharat spice and salt and cook until the meat has just browned (do not overcook). Remove from the heat, add the pomegranate molasses and mix through. Set to one side.

To make the dough, sift the flour into a large bowl and sprinkle with the yeast. Make a well in the centre of the bowl, pour 400ml water and the melted butter into the well and using your hands, begin incorporating the flour into the liquid from the outside edge to the inside edge until it all comes together. If the dough feels dry, slowly add the remaining 100ml water.

Turn the dough out onto a clean work surface and knead until it is smooth and pliable. Place into a bowl and leave to rest in a warm, draught-free place for 30 mins.

Heat the oven to 200°C.

Pull off a piece of dough about the size of an orange. Lightly dust a rolling pin with flour and roll out the dough as thinly as possible. Using a 10cm biscuit cutter, cut out circles in the dough. Place a tablespoon of the meat filling in the middle of the circle and spread it thinly, leaving about 1.5cm inch from the outside rim.

Spray a baking tray with oil and place the meat pies onto the tray. Let them rest for 20 mins before baking them.

Place the tray into the hot oven until the pies are cooked, around 12-15 mins.

Photography by @dearsafia
Styling by @dearsafia
Portrait by Imad Mortagy

SAMBOUSEK BIL JIBNEH (CHEESE PIE)

Donated by Maria Bizri of Pomegranate Kitchen
@pomegranatekitchenhk

"Syria holds a special place in my heart. I grew up walking the streets of Damascus. It's a place full of warmth and culture, depth and diversity. It's heartbreaking to see what is happening to Syria and its warm and generous people. There will be a generation of children that have grown up not knowing anything but refugee camps and war. For me, food is about culture and storytelling. I am grateful to have been asked to take part in this project and hope to continue to support the initiative while telling a story about a country that I love."

Serves 6

250g salted butter, melted
250g grated halloumi
200g mozzarella
100g parmesan
50g parsley, chopped
50g mint, chopped
2 tbsp toasted sesame
2 tbsp nigella seeds
pinch of chili powder
pinch of black pepper
1 packet of store bought filo

The Armenian community in the Levant has a huge culinary influence on the food of the area. Especially in a number of major cities such as Aleppo, Damascus and Beirut. I grew up eating similar pies, rich and buttery and filled with two or three local cheeses like Akawi and Mushalshalah (a cheese similar to halloumi in flavour, but knotted and stringy). In this recipe, I replaced these cheeses with the more readily available Parmesan and Mozzarella. I found these worked well and the Parmesan added a slight pepperiness to the dish. This is a very easy and rather surprising dish. It sounds a lot heavier than it is with cheese being the main ingredient - but the mint, parsley and hint of chili brighten the dish and contrast perfectly with the richness of the cheese.

Grate all three cheeses and mix with the herbs, pepper and chili in a bowl and set aside. Preheat your oven on to 180°C.

When working with filo, make sure you work fast so that the pastry doesn't harden and break. It's a really thin pastry and will harden when exposed to air, therefore, if you need to take your time, cover the pastry with a damp kitchen towel or fabric napkin while working.

To make individual pies, grease a ramekin and place one layer of filo at the bottom taking care to cover all the sides with the pastry. Brush the first layer with butter and repeat the process until you have 6 layers. Fill the ramekin with your cheese mixture and fold in the sides. Butter the pastry and cover with 2-3 more layers of filo. I like to crumple any excess filo into little flower shapes and top the pie with it, but this is completely up to you. Drizzle the top with a little more butter and sprinkle with toasted sesame and nigella seeds. You can also make this in a Pyrex or a deep oven pan (about 5cm deep) and serve as a shared starter, this would need you to use 6 sheets of filo for the top, as well as the bottom.

Place your pie dish or ramekins in the oven and cook for 10-15 mins until golden brown. Serve hot with a side of salad, a pomegranate molasses based dressing would work really well with this pie as the acidity will work really well with creaminess of the cheese and the nuttiness of the butter.

SAVOURY

Photography by Petra Greening
Styling by @pomegranatekitchenhk

LAMB S'FEEHA

Donated by Saima Khan of Hampstead Kitchen
@hampsteadkitchn

"Food has the power to heal and unite. I have visited and cooked at refugee camps and this campaign struck a chord with me. I had no idea the campaign would become as big as it has done, and it has been amazing to see it featured around the world. I loved how well my three recipes were re-created by people who bought the #CookForSyria book. It is an honour to provide a savoury recipe for this book."

Makes 20

1 pack puff pastry, cut into squares

½ kilo finely mince lamb (ask the butcher to get it from the leg)

1 small white onion, grated

glug of pomegranate molasses

½ cup labneh (strained yoghurt)

1 large tomato, diced and with the pips taken out

2 handfuls of toasted pine nuts

pinch of salt

pinch of ground cinnamon

sprinkle of freshly ground black pepper

melted butter for brushing

There are varieties of this recipe found in many countries around the Middle East. I ate this version while in Damascus many years ago, with a glass of a cool orange blossom water and mint drink. I think I must have had about twenty in one sitting. Often food made in these parts is measured by hands and eyes, so putting together a recipe is always a little hard for me as I tend to cook in the same way. It's a hit as a canapés or part of a Middle Eastern afternoon tea or served as part of a mezze spread. I also make mine with labneh to tenderise the meat.

To prepare and bake: Preheat oven to 180°C

Grate the onion & dice the tomato, toast the pine nuts.

Combine the lamb, grated onion, labneh, diced tomato, glug of pomegranate molasses, toasted pine nuts and spices.

Mix well in a bowl with your hands until everything is mixed and bound together.

Cut the puff pastry into 10cm squares.

Put the square pastry pieces on a baking tray lined with greaseproof paper.

Spoon 2 tablespoons of the lamb mixture onto each and spread to the corners of the pastry.

Brush the pastry sides with a little butter.

Bake 20-25 mins until the lamb is cooked and the pastry has turned a golden brown.

To serve: Serve either hot or cold.

Note: these can also be made smaller, as mini canapes.

Serve with Labneh on the side and drizzle pomegranate molasses with fresh mint and pomegranate seeds.

Serve this dish with other mezze items with dips and bread for a mezze style party.

Photography @allabouttheolive
Styling by Saima Khan
Portrait by @allabouttheolive

SAVOURY

MANOUSHI FLATBREAD; FREEKEH WITH OLIVES, TOMATOES & GARDEN HERBS, CUMIN HUMMUS DF

Donated by Damian Clisby of Petersham Nurseries
@petershamnurseries

"We are very fortunate in London to have access to such a variety of food. I think it is important that we remember that and that food can be a great tool for bringing us together in times of need."

Serves 8

For the Manoushi flat breads
355g plain flour

10g fresh yeast

5g salt

2g sugar

175 -200 ml warm water

1 tablespoon extra-virgin olive oil

½ tsp cumin seeds, toasted

½ nigella seeds, toasted

½ sesame seeds, toasted

½ rosemary leaves chopped

extra olive oil for brushing

For the freekeh
200g freekeh, cooked

100g nocellara olive, chopped

25ml olive oil

100g tomatoes, chopped

50g mint

50g parsley

For the cumin hummus
250g cooked chickpeas

35ml olive oil

8g cumin, ground

½ small clove garlic

2g maldon sea salt

½ lemon, large unwaxed

salt & pepper to taste

Bread brings us all together, so I was inspired to bake something very simple that could easily be shared. It's easy to forget that it's the simple things in life that are often the most important.

For the Manoushi flat breads
To the warm water add the olive oil, sugar and yeast; mixing together.

In a large bowl mix the flour & salt together, then slowly add the water mixture combining well.

Tip out onto a work surface and knead for 15 mins.

Return the dough to the bowl and cover with a damp cloth.

Leave to rest in a warm place for an hour.

Meanwhile combine the seeds & rosemary together.

Split the dough into 8 equal pieces.

Using a rolling pin roll out each piece until its approx. 3-5mm thick.

To bake: I like to cook the breads over hot coals. Roughly 2 mins each side. Remove from the heat, brush with olive oil and scatter of the rosemary & seeds.

For the Freekeh:
Mix all ingredients to gather and season to taste.

For the cumin hummus
Start by infusing the cumin in the olive oil with the garlic clove until the cooked. Blend the cumin and oil then add the rest of ingredients and blitz until smooth. Season to taste with the salt and finish with a squeeze of lemon.

FATAYER SABANECH (SPINACH) & JIBNEH (CHEESE)

Donated by Dalia Dogmoch Soubra
@daliaskitchen

"My family is Syrian, but I grew up in Europe. We used to visit family in Syria every year before the war broke out, which has now displaced my family and also kept me away from Syria since 2011. Keeping Syrian recipes alive has become a personal wish of mine, and this initiative strikes a very personal note for my entire family and me."

Makes 20 – 24 parcels

Dough

1 tsp active dried yeast
60ml warm water
400g flour
2 tsp salt
2 tbsp sugar
150ml lukewarm milk
60ml olive oil
A little melted butter to brush the pastry

Cheese filling

50g Akkawi or Kashkaval (cow) cheese (if unavailable use more of the cheeses below)
50g mozzarella
100g feta cheese
25g parsley, finely chopped
25g mint
1 beaten egg
2 tbsp olive oil

Spinach filling

1 onion, finely chopped
200g baby spinach, roughly chopped
50g chopped walnuts
1 tsp sumac
Rind of one lemon
¼ tsp grated nutmeg
½ tsp salt
½ tsp white pepper
1 beaten egg
2 tbsp olive oil

Fatayers are baked commonly in Middle Eastern homes, and even more so in Syrian families. There are so many variations of these, but I picked my favourite. They are also very representative of Syrian bakes and so I felt perfect for this book. Fatayers come in all shapes, including triangles and pockets. These oval shaped spinach and cheese parcels remind me of my family's Syrian kitchen.

Add the yeast to the warm water and let it sit for a few mins.

In a large bowl, combine flour, salt and sugar. Add the water with yeast, milk, and olive oil and knead. Add a little more flour or oil if it is too wet or dry. Knead the dough until smooth. Place in a bowl, cover with a towel, and let stand for 30 mins.

While the dough is resting make the fillings: Using a fork, combine the cheeses, parsley and mint. Add the beaten egg and oil, and combine well.

For the spinach filling, heat a pan with a little vegetable oil and sauté the onions until soft and translucent. Add the spinach, walnuts, sumac, lemon rind, nutmeg, salt and pepper and mix well. Cook the spinach mixture for a few mins, just until the spinach wilts. In a bowl add the egg and olive oil, and mix well.

Divide the dough in half, and set one piece aside. Roll out the dough into a 30cm or so round. Rub a little vegetable oil if you need to stretch out the dough more easily. Using a large round cookie cutter or the top of a glass, cut out round shapes. Repeat the process until you have used the all the dough. Flatten the cut outs by pressing gently with your hands into a slightly more oval shape, and place them on a non-stick baking tray. Fill the middle with 2 tablespoons of filling and pinch the opposite sides together to contain the filling.

Using a pastry brush, brush the edges with a little butter. Place the fatayers in the oven and bake them for 15 to 18 mins at 170°C or until the edge is slightly golden brown and serve warm.

SAVOURY

Photography by @sukainarajabali

SUBURAK CHEESE & PARSLEY BAKE

Donated by Dalia Dogmoch Soubra
@daliaskitchen

"My family is Syrian, but I grew up in Europe. We used to visit family in Syria every year before the war broke out, which has now displaced my family and also kept me away from Syria since 2011. Keeping Syrian recipes alive has become a personal wish of mine, and this initiative strikes a very personal note for my entire family and me."

Makes 9-12 portions

Cheese mixture
300g mozzarella
100g feta cheese
100g cow's milk kashkaval
60g parsley, finely chopped
½ tsp dried mint

Subarak
½ tsp salt
1 small onion, finely grated
1 egg
60ml clarified (may substitute with soft butter)
25ml vegetable oil
60ml warm milk
500g phyllo dough
500ml hot water

Optional
nigella seeds to garnish

Suburak is the king of buraks (Middle Eastern patties) in our home. It reminds me of a Syrian feast and our big family sitting around the table, so I have an emotional attachment to this recipe. Each household has a slight variation on the type of cheese used, but this recipe is the one the women in my family have always made. Please note: Akkawi cheese is typically used in this recipe, but as it is difficult to find outside the Middle East I substituted with Mozzarella.

Preheat your oven to 170°C.

Start by making the filling. Combine the cheeses with the parsley, mint, and salt and grated onion if you choose to include them. Set aside.

In a bowl, whisk the eggs, clarified butter, oil, and milk.

Once you unpack the filo sheets cover them with a damp towel to avoid drying them out. Prepare the hot water in a large, heat-proof container.

Brush a round, square or rectangular baking tray with the egg mixture and place two filo sheets on the bottom. No need to cut out the excess, let the sheets flow over if necessary. Using a pastry brush, brush the filo with the egg mixture.

Then add 3 – 4 heaped tablespoons of the cheese mixture on top.
Dip two of the filo sheets in the water, holding the edges with your fingertips. Submerge them for about 5 - 10 seconds making sure they soften but keep their shape.
Place the wet filo sheets on top of the cheese layer. Brush them with the egg mixture and add another layer of cheese.

Repeat the process until you have no cheese left.

For the top layer, do the same process with the phyllo sheets, but instead of spreading it straight, wrinkle the sheets. You will have to use more sheets to cover the last layer.

Fold any overflowing phyllo sheets over the top layer if necessary, and using your hands press the top layer slightly on to the bottom layers.

Pour the remaining egg mixture on top and sprinkle the top with nigella seeds.

You may slice the suburak before or after it comes out of the oven. Bake for 40 mins or until golden brown.

Once ready, cover with a clean towel so it does not dry out, and let it set for 5 mins before serving.

SAVOURY   Photography by @sukainarajabali

BRIOCHE STAR KADEH

Donated by Kathryn Pauline
@cardamom.and.tea

"I moved to Hong Kong a few months ago, and have been lucky enough to meet some wonderful people in the food world here. There are lots of #CookForSyria events happening this year, thanks to many contributors, chefs, and hosts, and especially Dervla Louli who organized most of them. #CookForSyria has such a beautiful mission—it's a wonderful thing to enrich the world with a deeper understanding of Syrian culture, while simultaneously raising money to aid survivors."

For the dough

1 ½ tsp yeast

½ tsp sugar

1 ½ tsp olive oil

57g 46°C / 115°F water

496g flour

1 tsp salt

73g granulated sugar

142g unsalted butter, melted and cooled

142g 46°C / 115°F whole milk (plus 1 or 2 tbsp more, if necessary)

For the martookhah (roux filling)

85g unsalted butter

1 tbsp granulated sugar

¼ tsp salt

77g flour

For shaping the star

dough

martookhah (roux)

3 tbsp pomegranate molasses

1 egg, beaten with 2 teaspoons water (egg wash)

1 tbsp white, untoasted sesame seeds

Kadeh is a roux-filled sesame-crusted brioche. It's a lesser known pastry because it's specific to the Assyrian diaspora, which is one thread in Syria's diverse cultural tapestry. So while my family is from all over the Middle East, my grandmother grew up in a village in Syria. She has fond memories of life on their farm, many of which involved enjoying kadeh with family. It's one of those desserts that's present at every special occasion, but also very much a part of everyday life. Kadeh is always on the lunch table to break the Advent fast, but it's also served to guests dropping in for a cup of chai.

For the dough
Combine the yeast, 1/2 teaspoon sugar, olive oil, and water in a bowl and stir to dissolve. Cover and let sit for 15 to 20 mins, until foamy.
Then add flour, salt, 73g sugar, melted butter, and milk. Combine everything and knead in the bowl to form a cohesive ball that doesn't stick to the sides (the dough will still be somewhat sticky and lumpy). If it looks dry, knead in a tablespoon of milk.
Shape into a ball, cover and rest for 1 hour.

For the martookhah
Melt the butter with the sugar and salt over a medium heat.
About 3 mins after the butter melts, add the flour and whisk continuously for 5-10 mins. The martookhah is ready once it is golden-brown; pull it off the heat when it's a shade lighter than you'd like it to be (it will keep cooking for a minute).
Cool to warm-room temp.

For the kadeh
Divide the dough into 5 equal pieces. Line a pan with baking paper.
Roll a piece out to shape it into a thin, smooth sphere with a 30 cm diameter.
To keep it from springing back, let it sit stick to the counter for 2 mins once it's rolled out.
Transfer to the lined pan.

Repeat, sandwiching the layers together like so: dough, warm martookhah, dough, pomegranate, dough, warm martookhah, dough, pomegranate, dough.

Brush the top with egg wash, sesame seeds, and chill for 20 mins exactly.
Mark a 7cm round in the centre. Use a sharp knife to cut a line from the outside edge of the round to the edge of the dough, and repeat to have 16 evenly-spaced slashes from the center.
Take 2 adjacent fringes of dough and twist them out 2 times, then pinch the ends together. repeat, and rest for 30 mins.

Preheat the oven to 175° C.

Bake for 30 mins, until the outside is deeply golden brown.

SAVOURY   Photography by @cardamom.and.tea

RYE MANOUSHI, SHANKLISH, APRICOT, AMARDEEN, ALEPPO CHILLI, MARJORAM

Donated by Johnnie Collins of Store Kitchen Studios
@johnniecollins

"This is the third #CookForSyria project I have been involved with and it's a real privilege. We had Imad from Imad's Syrian Kitchen with us for a week doing brunches and dinners in the summer and he taught us a great deal about Syrian food and flavours. It's a great feature of the hospitality industry that people are willing to donate extra time and energy for good causes and hopefully this book will have a direct impact on the lives of people in need of help."

6 Manoushi

9 nectarines cut into thin rounds along the stone (1 per bread, you could use apricots, plums

or pears depending on the season)

600g shanklish cheese, cut or crumbled (beenleigh blue would be a nice sub if you can't get this)

aleppo chilli

big bunch of fresh marjoram with flowers if possible

dried marjoram

100g walnuts, toasted and skins rubbed

juice of ½ lemon

Amardeen dressing

amardeen (dried apricot paste)

handful of toasted walnuts

dried marjoram

small clove of garlic, crushed

sea salt

chilli flakes

juice of ½ a lemon

olive oil

Manoushi

300g organic rye flour

100g spelt flour

1 tbsp of dried yeast

big pinch of salt

small pinch of sugar

approx. 200ml of warm water

50ml of olive oil

I don't really have a sweet tooth, nor am I much of a baker – so this is a savoury recipe requiring minimum baking skills. I love the mountain flavours found in some Syrian cooking and this dish is inspired by a recent trip to the mountains in Italy. At the top of a long trek I made a snack of fresh focaccia, apricots, salted ricotta, chilli flakes, olive oil and some thyme and its flowers I spotted and picked on the way up. It's a snack I have been recreating ever since and is adapted here with some Syrian flavours and Manoushi flat breads that work tremendously well.

Chop the amardeen paste and hydrate with a little water in a small bowl.

Blitz with the rest of the ingredients, adding a salt and chili first and then tasting as you go.

Don't blitz too hard as ideally you want some texture.

For the manoushi, mix flour, salt, sugar and yeast into a big bowl.

Add most of the warm water and olive oil mixing as you go - you want a sticky ball of dough so mix well.

Transfer to an oiled bowl and leave to sit covered in warmish place for around 2 hours, punch the air out of it, transfer to a floured work surface and portion into 6 and roll into 6 flat round breads.

Heat a frying or non-stick flat pan, and fry the breads individually on each side for 2-3 mins. It should puff up in places and have a some colour in places. Personally I like a few black bits.

Dollop the Amardeen dressing directly onto the breads, followed by the nectarine, cut Shanklish, a sprinkling of Aleppo chilli, olive oil and a sprinkling of sea salt. Add black pepper if you like. Good for a sharing starter or for a loving dinner or lunch with some fresh leaves on the side.

Photography by @CharlotteHuCo
Styling by @lily_vanilli_cake

SPICED LAMB PIES

Donated by Eric Lanlard of Cake Boy
@eric_lanlard

"Sadness is a major reason for taking part in this amazing campaign. I still find it difficult to understand how in today's world people can be so destructive. Such devastation in a beautiful country full of history is a tragedy. The pictures and reports of the terrible conditions faced by Syrian refugees are heartbreaking, especially considering how many children are involved. It was a no-brainer when I was asked to take part."

Serves 4

1 tbsp olive oil

1 red onion, finely chopped

1 garlic clove, crushed

2 tsp paprika

2 tsp ground cumin

1 tsp ground cinnamon

500g (1lb) minced lamb

400g (13oz) can of chopped tomatoes

1 tbsp tomato purée

410g (13½oz) can of chickpeas, drained and rinsed

50g (2oz) raisins

50g (2oz) dried apricots, chopped

2 tbsp fresh chopped mint

375g (12oz) ready or homemade puff pastry

Plain flour, for dusting

1 egg, beaten

½ tsp cumin seeds, lightly crushed

salt and freshly ground black pepper

These cute little pies are full of rich flavours. The spices and chickpeas are fabulous but my favourite part is the aroma in the kitchen of freshly crushed cumin seeds toasting while the pies bake. Utterly delicious!

Heat the oil in a large saucepan. Add the onion and garlic and fry gently over a low heat for 5 mins, until softened.

Add the ground spices and fry for 1 minute. Increase the heat slightly, add the lamb and stir-fry until browned. Stir in the chopped tomatoes, tomato purée, chickpeas, raisins, apricots and mint. Cover and simmer for 20 mins, stirring occasionally.

Meanwhile, preheat the oven to 200°C.

Season the mixture with salt and pepper, then divide between four 250ml (8fl oz) individual pie dishes and leave to cool.

Roll out the pastry on a lightly floured surface and cut out 4 discs slightly bigger than the diameter of the top of the pie dishes. Brush the rims of the dishes with some of the beaten egg, cover each pie with a pastry lid and trim off any excess.

Press the pastry edges against the rim of the dish to seal and crimp the edges. With a sharp knife, make several slashes across the centre of the pastry, but don't pierce all the way through.

Brush the pastry all over with beaten egg and sprinkle over the cumin seeds.

Place the dishes on baking trays and bake in the oven for 20 mins, or until puffed up and golden.

Photography by @KatieWilsonFoto
Styling by @clerkenwellboyec1
Portrait by @katewhitaker01
Bowls by @kanalondon

SPINACH FATAYER DF

Donated by Sandra Greiss
@sandra.greiss

"I find the initiative incredibly inspiring for many reasons. Food plays a big part in Middle Eastern culture and using it to raise money for a cause that is close to my home and heart means a lot to me. Children are our future and seeing the lives of Syrian children affected by war in their own country is heartbreaking. #CookForSyria not only raises the awareness of what is happening in Syria, it also gives us a chance to try and make a difference."

For the dough
360g of plain flour
250ml water
80ml olive oil
1 tbsp dry active yeast
1 tsp caster sugar
1 tsp salt

For the filling
600g of frozen spinach
4 tbsp of sumac
1 tbsp ground cinnamon
1 shallot or red onion
1 tsp salt
1/2 tsp black pepper
Handful of pine nuts (optional

Fatayer are a staple in many Middle Eastern homes. They are eaten for breakfast, as a snack during the day or even as a side dish at dinner. They can be vegan (like the spinach ones here) or filled with minced meat or cheese. Any leftover dough can be used for 'open fatayer', our version of pizza, without the cheese. The spinach ones are my favourite, probably because they remind me of spending time at my best friend's house growing up. Her mum made the best spinach fatayer and her secret was in the amount of sumac she used. Don't be surprised – it's what gives it a delicious tang.

Place the flour in a stand mixer bowl, along with the yeast, salt and sugar. Make a well in the middle and add most of the water and olive oil. With a dough hook attachment, mix the dough for at least 5 mins, until it springs back and doesn't feel sticky. Line a bowl with olive oil, place the kneaded dough in a bowl, cover and prove for a couple of hours.

Defrost the spinach and discard all the excess water/juice. Make sure all the moisture is squeezed out of the spinach – I use a sieve. Chop the onion very finely, add it to the spinach and mix well. Add the sumac, cinnamon, salt and pepper.

Preheat your oven at 200°C (fan).

Roll the dough out to roughly 2mm thick and using a 4-inch round cutter, cut as many dough circles as you can. Fill the middle of each cut-out dough with a tablespoon of the spinach mix. Bring together three sides of the dough to the centre and pinch well to create a triangle shape. Repeat until you run out of mixture and dough.

Place your spinach parcels on a baking tray, about 1cm apart, and into the oven. Bake for 13 to 15 mins, until golden.

Take out of the oven and leave to cool completely before attempting to eat them. Trust me, they're much tastier once cooled. Enjoy them on their own or dipped in hummus or baba ganoush. Sahtein!

Photography by @KatieWilsonFoto
Styling by @clerkenwellboyec1

WILTED HERB AND RICOTTA BOREK

Donated by Rebecca Oliver of Dusty Knuckle
@thedustyknuckle

"In a world that is so divided, it makes sense to revert to what makes us feel alive and connected as humans. For me, that has always been good food. Sharing stories and recipes creates magical spaces for local and global communication. I've always felt that eating and love go hand in hand, since my most memorable and enjoyable meals are those in comforting places with people I adore. While we cannot change the world through writing or buying this book, perhaps we can share more of this sentiment."

200g rocket

2 bunches coriander — washed, stalks included, root ends thrown away

2 bunches parsley — washed, stalks included, root ends thrown away

2 bunches mint — washed and picked, stalks thrown away

3 cloves garlic — finely chopped

50ml extra virgin olive oil

1 tsp of Turkish chilli flakes

3-4 pinches of Maldon sea salt

200g ricotta (or feta, or any other soft cheese)

3 tbsp of parmesan (or any hard cheese)

1 tbsp of sumac

1 tsp pine nuts — toasted in butter

300g puff pastry

2 tbsp of egg wash - 1 egg mixed well with a pinch of salt

1 tsp of mixed seeds (nigella, sesame, fennel)

Chicken hearts were on the menu during my first week at Moro, finished off with lemon and eaten with wilted herbs and yoghurt. Whilst typically Middle Eastern, cooking with an abundance of fresh herbs was completely new and amazing to me. I last made this dish at home when I had nothing in the fridge except for a bunch of sad-looking, wilted coriander, a tiny chunk of feta, and a random leaf from the Turkish Food Centre (which turned out to be mallow).

Filling
In order to make this correctly, you need the herbs and rocket to wilt and any water to evaporate, so they cook in oil rather than in their released liquid: think glossy al dente rather than sludgy Popeye spinach.

You need a large, heavy bottomed pan (approx. 30 cm). Place this over a low heat for two mins. When the pan is very hot, crank it up to full and throw in (all in one go) — your oil, greens, garlic, salt and chilli and stir so that all of the greens are coated in the oil. Add more oil if it looks a bit dry. Cook for around 5 mins, stirring occasionally, until it tastes sweet, but still has some bite to it.

Next, remove from the pan, drain if too wet and allow to cool. Chop it as fine as you like, then add ricotta, sumac, pine nuts and parmesan. Mix together and season to your taste.

Making the Borek
Making puff pastry is time consuming, but it is so rewarding that it really is worth it. If you complete fluff it, it will inevitably end up being rough puff, which is less layered but equally delicious. I advise looking up a 'how to' video online or buying a picture guide cookbook. Failing that, the shop bought puff will work fine.

Roll your pastry out in a rectangle 4mm thick. Then cut it into 10cm squares. In the middle of each place a dollop (roughly a tablespoon) of your filling. Fold into a triangle and seal the edges with the edge of your finger. Crimp the edges by pushing down with the back of a fork.

Refrigerate uncovered for at least thirty mins and preheat your oven to 180°C. (You can freeze them at this point too).

Using a pastry brush (or paint brush!), brush your egg wash liberally over the triangles. Decorate the edges with whatever spices and seeds you enjoy.

Bake for 20 mins or until golden.

Serve whilst hot with a bowl of seasoned yoghurt and thinly sliced red onions.

SAVOURY

Photography by @KatieWilsonFoto
Styling by @lily_vanilli_cake

COURGETTE & 3 CHEESE MAN'OUSHEH

Donated by James Walters of Arabica Bar & Kitchen
@arabicabarandkitchen

"I have a strong affinity with the cause. My involvement with #CookForSyria and #BakeForSyria followed on naturally from my own initiatives with the Soup for Syria campaign, which I launched at Arabica Bar & Kitchen after spending time in Lebanon in the Summer of 2015."

Makes: 4 x 6inch flatbreads

For the dough

250g unbleached strong white flour

5g salt

10g sugar

3g fresh baker's yeast (or 1½ g dry yeast)

120ml lukewarm water

10g olive oil

For the topping

1 large garlic clove

2 tbsp olive oil

75g mascarpone

1 courgette, thinly sliced into rounds

50g mozzarella, coarsely grated

50g halloumi, coarsely grated

½ red chilli, deseed and finely diced, optional

Sea salt

1 tbsp nigella seeds

40g ricotta

2 tbsp pine nuts

To serve

mint leaves

lemon zest

olive oil

Man'ousheh is a breakfast staple, eaten on the hoof and found in bakeries across the Levantine region. The thickness of the dough varies but the toppings are fairly standard with the most popular being Cheese or Za'tar or a combination of both. I have always adopted a playful approach to the Levantine kitchen, and while I love the traditional topping combinations, I equally enjoy mixing things up in a respectful and identifiable way. This summery rendition pays homage to a pizza bianco with plenty of eastern promise - from the salty halloumi cheese, toasted pine nuts, sprightly zest of a lemon and finished off with a few smacked fresh mint leaves. For the best results, I'd recommend buying a pizza stone.

In a large bowl, combine the flour and salt. In a separate bowl, add the sugar, yeast and half the water. Mix well to dissolve the sugar and yeast. Add the remaining water and olive oil and mix again.

Add the mixture slowly to the flour, until it's all incorporated, stirring in one direction to develop the glutens. Once the dough has come together and is too stiff to stir, turn it onto a lightly floured work surface and knead for 8-10 mins.

Clean out the large bowl, wipe dry and brush lightly with oil. Return the dough to the bowl, cover with clingfilm and leave to rise for 1½-2 hours, until approximately doubled in size.

Next, heat the oven to 180C. Wrap the garlic cloves in tin foil with 2 tbsp of olive oil and bake for 40 mins. Remove from the oven and leave to cool. Once cooled, squeeze the garlic cloves from the skin into the oil they were cooked in and mash with a fork. Add to the mascarpone and stir.

When the dough is ready, heat the oven to your hottest setting, ideally around 270C. Then gently punch the dough down, and turn it out onto a lightly floured surface. Cut the dough into 4 evenly sized pieces and work into balls. Leave to rest, covered for 10 mins.

Working with one piece at a time (keeping the others covered), flatten the dough ball out with the palm of your hand. Using a rolling pin, roll out the dough ball to around 15cm in diameter.

Evenly smear the mascarpone over the flatbread bases, leaving a 1cm border around the edge. Cover with courgette rounds, some mozzarella and halloumi. Sprinkle with chilli, sea salt and nigella seeds. Finally, add 3-4 blobs of ricotta, scatter with pine nuts and drizzle over a little olive oil.

Cook for 3-4 mins, or until the edges are crisp and golden. Remove from the oven and garnish with mint leaves and a little lemon zest.

Photography by @KatieWilsonFoto
Styling by @dearsafia
Portrait by @patricianiven

SPINACH BÖREK

Donated by James Walters of Arabica Bar & Kitchen
@arabicabarandkitchen

"I have a strong affinity with the cause. My involvement with #CookForSyria and #BakeForSyria followed on naturally from my own initiatives with the Soup for Syria campaign, which I launched at Arabica Bar & Kitchen after spending time in Lebanon in the Summer of 2015."

Makes 5 boregi or 10 canape size

To make the filling

250g spinach, washed, roughly chopped, squeezed to remove the water

200g feta cheese, crumbled

2 eggs, whisked

2 spring onions, finely sliced

1 tsp nigella seeds

¼ tsp ground nutmeg

2 tbsp dill stalk, finely chopped

1 tsp sea salt

½ tsp freshly ground black pepper

To make the boregi

5 filo pastry sheets

50g butter ghee (or clarified butter)

1 egg, whisked for the egg wash

poppy seeds

Garnish

fresh dill, chopped

Börek are much-loved pastries and pies of all shapes and sizes common throughout Turkey and the Balkans. Spinach börek is a nation-wide favorite, made for and served at afternoon tea gatherings, sold by street vendors or patisseries early in the morning for breakfast, or enjoyed as part of meal for lunch or dinner.

Preheat the oven to 190C/375F/gas mark 5 and line a large baking tray with baking parchment.

Add all the filling ingredients to a bowl, mix well and refrigerate for 30 mins before use. The egg will set and bind the filling together.

Open the packet of filo pastry. Lay them on dry surface and cover with a damp tea towel. This will minimise the chance of the ultra-thin pastry drying out and cracking when you roll it.

Working with one filo sheet at a time, place on a dry surface with the long edge facing you.

Roughly divide the filling in the bowl. Place the filling along the longest edge, leaving about 2cm of room at each end.

Carefully roll into a long sausage shape. Generously brush with butter ghee.

Gently arrange the long sausages into tight coils. Repeat for all 5 filo pastries.

Place on a baking tray and brush with the beaten egg and sprinkle with poppy seeds.

Bake for 30 mins or until golden brown.

Transfer to a serving dish and sprinkle with chopped dill.

Photography by @KatieWilsonFoto
Styling by @dearsafia

LAHMUCAN

Donated by James Walters of Arabica Bar & Kitchen
@arabicabarandkitchen

"I have a strong affinity with the cause. My involvement with #CookForSyria and #BakeForSyria followed on naturally from my own initiatives with the Soup for Syria campaign, which I launched at Arabica Bar & Kitchen after spending time in Lebanon in the Summer of 2015."

For the dough
500g strong white flour

170ml tepid water

2 tsp sugar

120g Greek-style yoghurt

2 tsp dried yeast

2 tbsp olive oil

2 tsp salt

For the lamb topping
250g shoulder of lamb, de-boned and minced

1 small onion, finely diced

2 cloves garlic, finely minced

1 tomato, finely diced

handful flat leaf parsley, finely chopped

2 tbsp pomegranate molasses

1 tbsp hot turkish red pepper paste (aci biber salcasi)

½ tsp cinnamon

½ tsp aleppo pepper flakes

1 tsp tomato puree

¼ tsp cumin, toasted, ground

¼ tsp freshly ground black pepper

¼ tsp allspice

¼ tsp nutmeg

1 tsp flaked sea salt

To garnish
flat leaf parsley

aleppo pepper flakes

Lahmacun is a spicy Levantine lamb pizza made with an aromatically spiced blend of finely ground beef or lamb, red peppers and tomatoes spread by hand onto the dough. I prefer the ultra-thin slightly spicier Turkish version. Locals tend to eat several in a single sitting with sprigs of parsley and a squeeze of lemon rolled into a wrap. For the best results, I'd recommend using a pizza stone.

In a large bowl combine the flour and salt. In a separate bowl add the sugar, yeast and the tepid water. Mix well to dissolve the sugar and yeast. Once dissolved add the remaining water, yoghurt and olive oil and mix well. Add this mixture slowly to the flour until all incorporated stirring in one direction to develop the gluten. Once the dough has come together and is too stiff to stir, turn onto a lightly floured work surface and knead for 10 mins and gently form into a ball. Clean out the bowl, wipe dry and brush lightly with oil. Return the dough to the bowl, cover with cling film and leave to rise for 1.5 – 2 hours, until approximately doubled in size.

Add the tomatoes, onion, garlic, tomato paste, pepper paste, pomegranate molasses, parsley and the spices to the minced lamb and mix well, it should be moist but not watery.

When the dough has doubled in size, knock back, and turn out onto a lightly floured surface. Cut the dough into 6 evenly sized pieces and work into balls. Leave to rest, covered with a dry cloth for a further 20 mins in a warm place.

Preheat the oven to your hottest setting. Ideally 300°C. If you are using a pizza stone remember to place it in the oven before switching it on. This will allow the stone to come up to temperature slowly, and minimize the risk of it cracking.

Roll each dough ball to approximately 8 inches in diameter. Place 2 tablespoons of the lamb mixture onto the center of the dough and gently spread until you have a thin even covering of meat with a ½ inch border around the edge. Sprinkle a few pine nuts on top.

Place in the oven and bake for 4-6 mins or until the crust is lightly browned.

Serve with lemon, fresh parsley and a pinch of Aleppo pepper

Photography by @KatieWilsonFoto
Styling by @lily_vanilli_cake

SYRIAN SOURDOUGH BIALY

Donated by Fergus Jackson of Brick House
@brickhousebread

"With a conflict that's so far away and so horrific, it's hard to understand how you can make a difference in a positive way. There's obviously nothing wrong with donating money – but doing so while being able to make something and be part of an event that celebrates and increases awareness of Syria's culture feels more constructive."

Makes 12

This recipe assumes you have a sourdough starter or 'mother' on the go from which you can make a liquid levain (100% hydration). If not, you can try substituting the sourdough portion of the recipe for 7g of dried baker's yeast and an extra 140g of both strong white bread flour and water, but it won't be quite the same.

For the dough
665g strong white bread flour

35g wholemeal bread flour

420g water, lukewarm

18g salt

280g ripe sourdough levain

For the filling
150g olives

6g aleppo pepper

8g za'atar, plus more for sprinkling

50ml olive oil, plus more for finishing

100g feta

zest of 1 lemon

We developed this recipe for the first #BakeForSyria event on Columbia Road in July 2017. A bialy is basically a bagel with a dimple instead of a hole, which in this case we stuffed with Syrian flavours including olives, Aleppo pepper and za'atar. Perfect for breakfast with a strong cup of black coffee!

Put all your ingredients in a bowl and mix by hand to form a shaggy dough. Scrape this dough into a well-oiled bowl, cover with cling film and set aside at room temperature. As this dough hasn't been heavily mixed or kneaded, it needs about 2 hours to develop and ferment.

Meanwhile, fold the dough every 30 mins (3 times in total). I'll explain what I mean by this. If you imagine your dough as a square, you're going to take each 'side' of it and stretch it slightly upwards, and then fold it back on top of itself. Fold the dough 4 times (once for each 'side'), and then flip the dough over so the folds you've made are now underneath. The dough will be pretty sticky, so make sure your hands are wet while you do this.

After each fold, you'll notice small changes in the dough that show it's gaining strength. It will start to feel stronger, smoother and gassier. By the time you've done your third fold it should be slightly shiny and 'sitting up' in the bowl.

During breaks in folding, mix the filling. In a small bowl add the olive oil, Aleppo pepper, lemon zest and za'atar and mix to form a loose paste. Remove any stones and then roughly chop the olives and add to the bowl. Finally, crumble in the feta, gently mix all the ingredients together and set aside.

Half an hour after the final fold, turn the dough out onto a work surface, and divide into 12 pieces, each around 110g. Shape each of these into tight balls and place evenly spread out on a lightly oiled baking tray (probably over 2 trays, 6 dough balls per tray). Very lightly sprinkle with flour, and then cover with a tea towel and leave to prove.

Turn on oven to 225°C and place an empty baking tray in the bottom.

After an hour and a half, maybe more, the dough balls should have grown in size, spread out, and look bubbly. Make a dimple in the centre of each ball with your thumb, and then fill with a good heaped teaspoon of the spiced olive mix. Finally brush the outer rim of each ball with olive oil, and sprinkle with za'atar.

Place in the oven, but before closing the door, throw a few ice cubes into the empty baking tray at the bottom to create some steam.

Bake for 15 mins and allow to cool slightly. They are best enjoyed still oven warm.

Photography by @KatieWilsonFoto
Styling by @dearsafia

CHARD AND FETA BOUREKAS WITH POMEGRANATE JAM AND LABNEH

Donated by Bill Granger of Granger & Co.
@bill.granger

"The brilliant #CookForSyria and #BakeForSyria campaigns have inspired chefs from all walks of life to rally together and raise awareness and money for Syria's children, while ensuring the legacy and beauty of Syria's food lives on. Of course, I wanted to play my small part in this."

Makes 20 bourekas

6 swiss chard leaves, stalks diced and leaves shredded

4 cloves garlic

1 tbsp coriander seed

1 tbsp cumin seed

1 tbsp fennel seed

1 tbsp mustard seed

¼ bunch parsley, chopped

½ bunch coriander, chopped

¼ bunch dill, chopped

200g feta cheese, crumbled

1 tbsp sumac, plus 1 tsp extra for sprinkling

½ nutmeg, grated

1 tsp dried mint

150 ml olive oil, plus extra for oiling filo pastry

1 lemon, juiced and zested

1 packet filo

1 egg, lightly beaten, for egg wash

1 tsp black sesame

1 tsp white sesame

1 tsp ground cinnamon

To serve

Pomegranate jam

Labneh (or yoghurt)

For the pomegranate jam

2 tsp pectin

4 cups sugar

4 cups pomegranate juice

2 lemon

2 cup pomegranate seeds

I'm a sucker for any savoury pie and this is my take on the common pastry, boureka. Mine are filled with chard and feta and I serve them with creamy labneh and punchy pomegranate jam. These are easy to put together using shop bought filo pastry. You can also double the recipe and fill the freezer. I love eating these at any time of the day but they're especially good as part of a mezze Sunday brunch, alongside a big chopped salad, dips, crudités and pickles.

For the bourekas
Preheat the oven to 180°C.

Place the chard stalks, garlic and spices in a frying pan over a medium heat and sweat until chard stalks are translucent. Add the shredded leaves and cook through until the mixture starts to dry out. Remove from the heat and add the chopped herbs and feta. Mix well and season with sea salt and 1 tablespoon sumac, nutmeg, dried mint, and then add the olive oil, lemon juice and lemon zest.

Lay two sheets of pastry out and cut into three strips lengthways. Oil well between sheets and place a 75g portion of the mixture in each line. Fold from corner to corner, creating triangles.

Place bourekas on a baking paper lined baking tray, brush with egg, sprinkle with sesame seeds and bake for 20 mins until light golden brown.

Remove from oven and place on a serving platter or plates. Sprinkle with extra sumac and cinnamon and serve with a dollop of pomegranate jam and labneh (or yoghurt).

For the pomegranate jam
Mix the pectin and 1 tablespoon of sugar and set aside.

Boil the juice and remaining sugar together for 15-20 mins or until reduced by 1/3. Dissolve the pectin mixture in 3 tablespoons of the reduced liquid. Combine this mixture with the remaining reduced liquid, add the lemon juice and cook for a further 5 mins. Add the pomegranate seeds and leave to cool and set.

Store any remaining jam in the fridge.

Photography by @KatieWilsonFoto
Portrait by Mikkel Vang

TURCOMAN-INSPIRED SOURDOUGH FLATBREAD

Donated by E5 Bakehouse
@e5bakehouse

"At E5 bakehouse we are big fans of Syrian and Middle Eastern flavours. We've also seen first hand how cooking and baking can unite people and start conversations both through our Just Bread Refugee project run in collaboration with the Refugee Council, and at the Syrian Supper Club regularly run by the Hands up Foundation at our bakery. Getting involved with #BakeForSyria is an opportunity for us to help make a difference."

Makes 12 flatbreads of 150g each

Preparation of the leaven
100g rye starter
870g milk
200g strong white flour
187g wholemeal flour

Preparation of the dough
400g white flour
180g wholemeal flour
17g salt

When we started experimenting to find a good flatbread recipe to make with our refugee bread class we were looking for a bread to serve with Middle-Eastern slow-cooked beef. This recipe worked out the best. The original comes from a 1995 book 'Flatbread and Flavors: A baker's Atlas' by Jeffrey Alford and Naomi Duguid. It is a Turcoman bread from Turkmenistan in Central Asia which uses yeast and goat's milk. We translated the recipe into a sourdough version (without yeast) using cow's milk. The final bread has a rich taste of milk because of the way the leaven is made and left to ferment for 24 hours.

Prepare the leaven by mixing all the ingredients together, cover and leave at room temperature for 24 hours.

To make the dough, mix all the ingredients with the leaven combining well until the dry ingredients are incorporated.

Wait 30 mins and then fold the dough for the first time (this is done by gently folding the dough over on itself in the bowl 4 times, turning the bowl 90 degrees after each fold). Repeat this process twice more at half hour intervals.

Cut the dough into 300g pieces and roll into balls. Cover.

Half each ball and flatten using a small quantity of flour to obtain a flatbread shape about 2 cm thick.

Rest for 20 mins.

The original recipe recommends stamping the flatbread before you bake to stop the bread from ballooning. In practice we noticed the bread comes out really well even when it has puffed up in the oven.

Bake at 250/300°C for less than 10 mins. You can adapt the time of the bake depending on how you like your flatbread. A short bake will keep the bread nice and moist. But the recipe works also well for a flatbread which is a bit darker and crunchy.

Keep covered for freshness

6. DESSERTS

—

ROAST FIGS, PISTACHIOS & SEMOLINA CAKE & KADAÏF

Donated by Pierre Sang Boyer of Pierre Sang
@pierre_sang

"Gastronomy is about being open to the world. It is important to share with people who are in need."

Serves 6

Roast figs
12 black figs
60g Acacia honey
200g water
1/2 vanilla bean
2 tsp orange blossom

Yoghurt ice cream
200g water
200g yoghurt
90g sugar
30g glucose

Kadaïf
80g kadaïf noodles
15g honey
30g olive oil
1 pinch of salt

Lemon and olive oil cream
30g egg whites
40g egg yolks
45g sugar
45g lemon juice
30g softened butter
25g olive oil

Pistachios & semolina cake
75g pistachios powder
25g semolina
150g sugar
2 eggs
20g flour
2g salt

I was inspired by traditional Syrian desserts. They remind me of family values and simple cuisine made with love and to share. I created this dessert using honey, yoghurt, kadaïf, pistachios and semolina. To me, these ingredients reflect perfectly the gastronomic heritage of the country.

For the roast figs
Make a syrup with honey, water and vanilla. Add the figs and cook for 25 mins at 180°C. Keep the cooking juice and add 10g of orange blossom water to make a delicate honey sauce.

For the yoghurt ice cream: Make a syrup with water, sugar and glucose. Let cool and mix with yoghurt. Use an ice-cream machine to churn it into ice cream.

For the kadaïf
Emulsify the honey and olive oil and coat the kadaïf noodles evenly. Bake in a preheated oven at 170°C until golden brown, turning occasionally to ensure even coloration.

For the lemon and olive oil cream
Whisk the eggs together with the sugar in a bowl. Heat the lemon juice in a pot and pour into the egg and sugar mixture until homogenous. Pour the mixture back into the pot and cook to obtain a smooth lemon curd. Keep in a container and cool to a temperature of about 45°C before incorporating the softened butter and olive oil with an immersion blender. Let the mixture sit in the refrigerator for at least 3 hours before serving.

For the pistachio and semolina cake: Mix all the ingredients together and pour in a mould. Cook at 180°C for 15 mins.

Photography by @alleycat_photograph
Portrait by @alleycat_photograph

PISTACHIO STUDDED CHOCOLATE BROWNIE PUDDING WITH A SALTED DATE CARAMEL AND PISTACHIO, ALMOND AND ROSE PETAL BRITTLE

Donated by Paul A Young of Paul A Young Fine Chocolates
@paul_a_young

"I got involved with #BakeForSyria primarily because it's a great cause, but also because it's a lovely way to offer support in a time of crisis. Cooking for the people you love is an age-old way of showing that you care, so what better way than to share these recipes and spread the message through baking."

Serves 10

Brownie pudding

100g unsalted (sweet) butter

250g unrefined caster sugar

75g golden syrup (you can substitute light corn syrup)

275g Guittard 74% chocolate organic baking wafers (or good quality 70% dark chocolate chips)

4 medium size free range eggs

70g plain (all-purpose) flour

100g of shelled pistachios, chopped

Date puree

250g pitted dates

150ml water

Salted caramel sauce

100g salted butter

100g unrefined light muscovado sugar

100g double (heavy) cream

1 tsp Maldon (flaked) sea salt

Almond, pistachio and rose brittle

1 tbsp honey

1 tbsp unrefined caster sugar

½ tsp Maldon (flaked) sea salt

50g shelled pistachio

50g flaked almonds

small handful of dried edible rose petals

This recipe comes simply from my love of chocolate puddings. I love the idea of setting this down in the middle of the table and everyone diving in together. The combination of dates, pistachio and rose petals gives this fudgy pudding a distinctly Middle-Eastern feel. I love the way the date caramel gives a wonderful depth of flavour when balanced against the rich chocolate and toasted pistachios. I'd serve this up with some rose water crème fraiche.

For the pudding
Melt together the butter, sugar and syrup until it bubbles.

Remove from the heat and add the chocolate and mix well.

Add the eggs and beat all until smooth, then add the flour and nuts, mixing well.

Pour into a 15cm deep baking dish and bake at 175°C/350°F/Gas Mark 3.5 for 25 to 30 mins.

It should still have a wobble when it leaves the oven. Don't leave it in the oven for any longer than the listed time so that the brownie middle is still soft and molten.

For the date puree
Chop the dates and simmer for 2 mins in the water. Blend until smooth.

For the caramel
Bring the butter, sugar and 100g of date purée to a simmer with the salt and cook for 3 mins.

Take off the heat, add the cream and mix well.

While still warm pour it over the brownie pudding and leave to stand.

For the brittle
On a flat baking tray, cook the pistachios and almonds in the oven at 170°C/330°F/Gas Mark 3 for 5 mins or until golden brown.

In a saucepan bring the honey, sugar and sea salt to a simmer until golden.

Throw in the nuts and stir to coat in the caramel.

Pour on to a sheet of parchment paper, sprinkle with rose petals and allow to cool.

Once cold, chop and break into pieces.

Sprinkle over the pudding and serve.

DESSERTS

Photography by @KatieWilsonFoto
Styling by @paul_a_young

PRESERVED LEMON PAVLOVA GF

Donated by Anna Higham of Lyle's
@lyleslondon

"Some close friends of mine spent time last year working with kids in a refugee camp on a Greek Island. Hearing about their time there and the stories of the young people they met really drove home the sheer enormity of the Syrian crisis for me. I'm so pleased to be involved in #BakeForSyria and make a small contribution with this recipe."

Serves 15

For the meringue
5 egg whites
40g preserved lemon vinegar
Pinch of fine salt
330g caster sugar
zest of 4 lemons

For the lemon puree
8 lemons
caster sugar
50g butter
pinch of salt

To serve
500ml double cream

We spend a lot of time preserving, pickling and fermenting at Lyle's and packing lemons into vinegar gives the most wonderful sweet, sour, salty and aromatic result. This pavlova was inspired by a dish at Lyle's using preserved lemon vinegar meringues and Meyer lemon sherbet. It captures those Middle Eastern qualities of being vibrant, surprising and balanced.

For the preserved lemons
Cut a deep cross into each lemon starting at the tip and going about 3/4 of the way down. Open up slightly, and pack with coarse salt. Tightly pack them with more coarse salt in a jar, making sure they are completely covered. Leave somewhere cool and dark for 6 months.

For preserved lemon vinegar
Rinse any salt from your preserved lemons, put into a sterilised jar and cover with cider vinegar. Leave in a dark cool place for a month.

Put egg whites, salt and vinegar into the bowl of a mixer and whisk on low speed. To build a strong meringue you want to whip the egg whites at a slower speed for a longer amount of time. Once at soft peaks add roughly 1/3 of the sugar and carry on whisking. Add the remainder of the sugar in thirds, fully incorporating between additions. Once the sugar has fully dissolved and you have a strong, shiny and thick meringue add the zest. Spread into a circle on a lined baking tray and bake at 140°C for 4 hours. The outside should be crisp and set but the inside will be similar to marshmallow. Allow to cool.

For the lemon purée
Zest 4 of the lemons and save. Keep flesh for later and put skin, pith and peel into a pan, covering with cold water. Bring to a boil then strain. Repeat twice with cold water each time. Weigh how much you have and add half of its weight in caster sugar. Cover with water and simmer on a low heat until peel is very soft. Strain the peel saving the liquid. Blend cooked peel with salt and butter adding enough cooking liquor to make a smooth, thick puree. Add sugar to taste, it should be a little bitter and not too sweet. Allow to cool.

Whip the cream with a little sugar to soft peaks and ripple through the lemon puree. Spoon this on top of the meringue. Segment the lemons, trying to get as little of the membrane as possible. Either blow torch the segments or put into a dry, very hot pan to char one side. Lay them over the cream and sprinkle over the lemon zest.

DESSERTS

Photography by @CharlotteHuCo
Styling by @lily_vanilli_cake

CHARGRILLED PLUMS, SWEET (SOYA) LABNEH AND TOASTED PLUM KERNELS GF, DF, V

Donated by Tom Hunt
@tomsfeast

Serves 2

200g yoghurt (soya, coconut etc)

3 tbsp date or maple syrup, plus more for serving

3 plums or other soft fruit, cut in half, seeds removed and kept

2 mint or sorrel leaves, rolled up and cut into thin shreds

My mission is to cook holistically considering nutrition, flavour, the environment and people involved in the production of our food. This has led me to invent a style of cooking which I call Root to Fruit Eating, which focuses on local-seasonal fruit and vegetables but celebrates the incredible ingredients available worldwide like Aleppo pepper and date syrup. This dish is best made when plums are in season, ripe and juicy. The plums are cooked whole and even the kernels are used. Allow the grilled plums to burn slightly, creating a bitter sweet flavour explosion.

Six hours in advance or the night before, strain the yoghurt through a piece of muslin or cloth inside a sieve to thicken it up. When ready, mix in a tiny pinch of salt and tablespoon of date or maple syrup.

Using a nutcracker, crack open the plum pips and remove the kernels. Toast the kernels in a hot, dry pan for 3-5 mins until slightly browned. Crush lightly in a pestle and mortar and put to one side.

Glaze the plums with a light drizzle of date or maple syrup. Place them on a hot griddle and allow to caramelise and char slightly then flip over and grill for a further minute.

To serve, place three plum halves on each plate with a big spoon of sweetened labneh, a drizzle more syrup, toasted kernels and shredded mint or sorrel.

Photography by @CharlotteHuCo
Styling by @lily_vanilli_cake

ROZ BHALEEB WITH POACHED QUINCE, HONEY SYRUP AND SWEET FENNEL AND ROSE DUKKAH GF, DF

Donated by Sarah Lemanski of Noisette Bakehouse
@noisettebakehouse

"The ethos of cooking, sharing and nourishing with generosity and love is ingrained in the culture of Middle Eastern countries. This sentiment is universal, ultimately creating comfort and doing what all good food should do: bringing people together. It is great that this initiative can support that ethos while bringing help to Syrians affected by the conflict."

Serves 4

75g pudding rice
400ml coconut milk (tinned)
450ml oat milk*
8 cardamom pods, crushed but not ground
1 vanilla pod
25g Demerara sugar
¼ + ⅛ tsp sea salt

*Look out for 'Barista' quality oat milk, it is thicker than most conventional oat milk drinks and provides a consistency more akin with whole milk. Of course you can use whole milk in place if dairy free is not a prerequisite.

For the poached quince
1 quince, peeled, quartered and cored.
150ml water
30g caster sugar

For the orange blossom syrup
2 tbsp honey (naturally set)
1 tbsp orange blossom water
2 tsp water

Roz Bhaleeb and Riz B Haleeb are Middle Eastern variants of rice pudding and this version uses a blend of coconut and oat milk, both of which lend an creaminess and natural sweetness. I like to top the cardamom and vanilla infused rice with perfectly poached quince and honey syrup for an elegant dessert, or serve a comforting bowl for breakfast on a cold morning, topped with yoghurt and fresh fruit. Either way the sweet dukkah should be obligatory, adding more complex layers of flavour and texture to a humble dish.

For the Roz Bhaleeb
Preheat the oven to 150°C.
Rinse the pudding rice to remove excess starch then place in a saucepan with the coconut and oat milk. Add the crushed cardamom pods and vanilla pod, its scraped out seeds and the Demerara sugar.
Bring to a boil then reduce to a simmer and cook for 25 mins. Stir every 5 mins to stop rice sticking to the pan.
After 25 mins, remove the cardamom and vanilla pods and pour mixture into an ovenproof dish that will hold at least 1.5 pints, place in the oven (uncovered) for 30 mins.

While this cooks, poach the quince and prepare the orange blossom syrup. (See below).

Once the pudding has baked, remove from the oven and cool for 15 mins, The longer you leave it the thicker and creamier it gets.
To serve, divide between four bowls and top with the quince, honey syrup and sweet dukkah (see recipe).

For the Poached Quince
Place the water and sugar in a saucepan large enough. Place to dissolve sugar, then add the quince - fully covered with water. If they are not, then simply top the pan up with a little more water.
Bring to the boil then reduce to a simmer and gently poach the quince until soft enough to be easily pierced with a sharp knife. Place a sieve over a bowl and drain the quince from its water, retaining it for the orange blossom syrup, (recipe below).
Allow to cool then cut each quarter into slices or cubes, to be used to top the rice pudding. I like to cut into small cubes to ensure a mouthful with every bite.

For the orange blossom syrup: Place ingredients in a pan and bring to the boil, reduce to a simmer for 1 minute, then remove from the heat.

Photography by @noisettebakehouse
Portrait by @helenadolby

DAMASK ROSE PRESERVE GF

Donated by Gregoire Michaud of Bakehouse
@gregoiremichaud

"Years before the war started, I had the chance to work for several weeks with Chef Mohamed Helal from Aleppo. I was struck by his passion, his contagious smile and his love of food: he told me all his cooking skills were passed down from his mother in the most authentic Aleppean tradition. When he invited me to take part in #BFS I was instantly moved. I am not doing this just for Chef Helal, but for all those people he represents in the hope that our efforts will help Syrian people re-establish peace and stability."

Damask rose preserve
300g damask rose
300g granulated sugar
half a tsp of citric acid

Frozen sheep yoghurt
500g sheep yoghurt
100g white sugar
the juice and zest of 1 lemon
a pinch of salt

Chef Helal taught me how to make one of the most intriguing foods around: Damask rose preserve. When he told me to use Damask rose petal, sugar and a pinch of "lemon salt" I looked at him in awe. I asked myself how we could make a jam without water and without cooking! This recipe is yet another reminder that mastering simplicity is often the most difficult.

For the damask rose preserve
Wash the rose petal (use untreated Damask roses if possible).
Mix the citric acid with the granulated sugar.
In a clean glass jar, build layers of petals and sugar until the jar is full.

Close the jar and leave it for about a week to 10 days at room temperature.

The mixture will diminish in volume, you can top the jar with more rose petals and sugar (1 to 1 ratio) until the jar is full.

Once done, the preserve takes the form of a jam and you can store it in the fridge.

For the frozen sheep yoghurt
Mix all the ingredients and churn it in your ice cream maker.

Keep in the freezer.

Serve a large scoop of frozen sheep yoghurt with the rose petal preserve and some chopped pistachios.

DATE SYRUP AND ORANGE BLOSSOM SPONGE PUDDING

Donated by Elly Curshen of The Pear Cafe
@ellypear

"What #CookForSyria achieved was truly incredible and I'm proud to have been involved. I'm absolutely thrilled to be asked to join in with #BakeForSyria: raising money and awareness for an important cause through the power of cake!"

serves 4

100g unsalted butter, softened plus extra to grease dishes

100g caster sugar

2 eggs

100g self-raising flour

zest of 1 orange, finely grated

2 satsumas/clementines/ small oranges, peel and pith removed and sliced 0.5-1cm thick (use the two best fit slices from each orange and eat the rest!)

1 tbsp orange blossom water

40g date syrup

80g golden syrup

Greek style yoghurt, to serve

A delicious, simple little cake that can be in front of you in less than half an hour? The dream, right! I'm an impatient baker and although I adore traditional steamed syrup pudding, I love these fast mini ones even more. I've used some classically Syrian flavours in a traditionally British pudding. The yoghurt contrasts well with the date syrup and orange while the fragrant orange blossom water makes this both familiar and new at once.

Preheat oven 200°C

Cream the butter and sugar really well in a mixer until light and fluffy.

Add the eggs one at a time, along with a spoon of flour, blending well. Fold in the rest of the flour and the orange zest.

Butter 4 individual pudding dishes.

In a small saucepan, gently warm together the two syrups and the orange blossom water and then divide between the 4 dishes. Lay a slice of orange in the base of each one on top of the syrup mixture.

Carefully spoon the cake mixture on top of the syrup (approx 100g in each).

Cover the dishes with buttered foil with a fold to allow for expansion. Make sure the edges are tightly sealed. Bake for 20 mins - until a skewer comes out clean.

Serve with Greek style yoghurt and an extra drizzle of date syrup.

Photography by @KatieWilsonFoto
Styling by @dearsafia

SOUR CREAM CARAMEL CORN BREAD PUDDING WITH PISTACHIO, ROSE AND HALVA

Donated by Gabriel Pryce of Rita's
@ritasdining

"Ever since the civil war in Syria began, the civilian death toll has been horrific. If we are going to continue to enjoy the flavours of the Middle East and the Arabic world, flooding our Instagram accounts with pictures from our favourite Levantine restaurants, buying cookbooks that espouse the joys of the spice markets in Bethlehem or holidaying by the coasts of the Dead Sea, we must in turn support those that have been affected by the horrific wars in the Middle East."

Cornbread
225g butter
225g sugar
285g polenta
50g flour
3 whole eggs
1 tsp baking powder
salt

Custard
120g butter
500ml milk
200g caster sugar
1 vanilla pod sliced open and seeds released
5 large eggs
pinch of Maldon sea salt

Sour cream caramel
250g caster sugar
125g butter
125ml sour cream

Rose cream
250 ml double cream
2 tbsp caster sugar
2 tbsp crushed rose petals
2 tsp rose water
1 tsp beetroot powder

Garnish
200g toasted pistachios
4 tbsp dried rose petals
150g Halva for grating
1 lemon for zesting

This is a sweet, indulgent and delicious dessert. It's essentially a bread and butter pudding with a twist – a lot of twists. It is a great ending to a large family meal, best served piping hot doled out of a casserole straight from the oven.

Preheat your oven to 170°C.

Cream the softened butter and the sugar together in a stand mixer with a whisk attachment. Once combined, whisk in one egg at a time, then stir in all the dry ingredients. Once well combined, pour the batter into a buttered baking dish and bake for 45 mins at 170°C. Remove the cornbread to cool on a rack.

Leave the oven on 170°C.

Cut the cooled cornbread into 3 inch pieces and place in a deep buttered baking dish.

For the Custard
Melt the 120g of butter in a large saucepan and brown over a high heat.

Remove from the heat and whisk in the milk, sugar, vanilla and salt until the sugar has dissolved, then whisk in the eggs.

Pour this custard over the cornbread and bake, covered for 30 mins, then uncovered for a further 25.

While this is baking make the rest of the components for the dish.

For the Caramel
Melt 250g caster sugar in a large flat bottomed pan, once it starts to melt stir with a spatula until it is all meted. When the bubbling sugar is a nice golden brown, stir in the butter. Remove from the heat and stir in the sour cream.

For the Rose Cream:
Place all ingredients in a large bowl and whisk until firm peaks are formed. Transfer to a piping bag with a flat round nozzle.

Assemble
Cut a large hunk of the baked cornbread pudding, being careful to keep some of the custard so each serving has a good amount. Pipe the pink rose cream atop each serving, drizzle with the caramel sauce, scatter with the pistachios and use a microplane or small grater to shave halva and lemon zest liberally over everything.

Photography by @KatieWilsonFoto
Styling by @lily_vanilli_cake

CARROT AND CARDAMOM MARMALADE GF, DF, V

Donated by Kylee Newton
@newtonandpott

"The reason I got involved with #BakeForSyria is because of its emphasis on raising awareness. It's not just about giving money. When someone makes a meal or a cake from one of the recipe books they are engaging with the issue. They are making a choice to think about the problems in Syria and this is how change can happen. Sometimes it's not only about giving a donation, but getting to know the issues at stake."

Makes 7-8 x 250ml jars.

1.5kg carrots

2 oranges

2 lemons

¼ tsp ground cinnamon

4 cardamom/smashed

1 kg granulated sugar

900ml water

20ml freshly squeezed lemon juice

At Newton & Pott we hate waste: our ethos is to 'Waste not, Want not' and this helps us to get the most out of our fruit and vegetables. This recipe is a great reflection of that and was created to use up all the leftover carrot bits that don't make it into our Whisky Pickled Carrots. Carrots blend perfectly with cardamom giving the marmalade a Syrian inspired twist. It's a marmalade you can use for sweet or savoury.

Wash, peel and grate the carrots, place in a large bowl.

Wash and cut the oranges and lemons in half and juice, keeping the rind.

Cut the rind in half again (making wedges) and with a teaspoon carefully scrape off the white pith. Once cleaned, slice the skins into long strips about 2-3mm wide.

Add the citrus juice and rind strips to the grated carrot and stir through the cinnamon, the gently smashed cardamom pods and sugar.

Cover with a tea towel and leave in the fridge to macerate overnight.

The next day, sterilise your jars and lids by washing in soapy hot water and rinsing thoroughly. Drip dry upside down then place into a warm oven set at fan oven preheated to 100°C for at least 20 mins.

Place the carrot citrus mix into a large mouthed pan (or jam/mason pan) with 900ml of water and the remaining lemon juice and bring to a hard rolling boil on a high heat.

Once boiling, lower heat a little but keep on the boil, stirring intermittently at first but more frequency towards the end so it doesn't stick and burn for about 40-50 mins or until the liquid has reduced and it's a thicker spreadable consistency.

When ready, ladle into your warm dry sterilised jars and seal while chutney is still hot. When cool, label and date.

Storage
Keeps sealed for up to 12 months. Once opened, keep in the fridge and eat within 6 months.

Photography by @KatieWilsonFoto
Styling by @newtonandpott

ROSE SCENTED PANNA COTTA, PISTACHIO, CURRANTS, RASPBERRIES, KATAIFI PASTRY

Donated by Peter Gilmore of the Quay Restaurant
@chefpetergilmore

"I feel that most people around the world realise that many innocent people have been caught up in the tragedy of the conflict in Syria. Being able to help by contributing a recipe or taking part in a dinner which raises funds to help the Syrian people is my small way of contributing to the worldwide relief effort."

Serves 10

500ml milk

80g caster sugar

3ml rose water

1 vanilla bean

250ml whipping cream

2 platinum grade gelatine leaves

250g fresh raspberries

150g fresh currant grapes

100g fresh or dried pistachio nuts

100g kataifi pastry (shredded pastry)

1 tbsp honey

2 tbsp melted butter

2 tbsp icing sugar

While travelling in the Middle East in my early 20s, I remember the wonderful pastry shops with their heady aromas of rose water and honey and the syrup soaked pastries topped with pistachio nuts. These memories inspired this elegant yet simple dessert, in which soft luscious rose-scented panna cotta is teamed with the crisp texture of honey roasted kataifi pastry. The addition of fresh raspberries, pistachio and currants add colour and bursts of flavour.

Place the milk, sugar, split and scraped vanilla bean and rose water in a small saucepan and bring to just below boiling point.

Take off the heat, whisk well and allow to infuse for 5 mins.

Soak the gelatine leaves in cold water for 5 mins. Strain out the milk mixture into a clean saucepan and discard the vanilla bean. Re-heat the milk until it reaches simmering point, remove from the heat, squeeze the water out of the gelatine leaves and add to the milk mixture. Whisk in well and chill the mixture over an ice bowl.

In the meantime, whip the cream to soft peaks and line ten dariole moulds with cling film. Once the milk mixture is cold but before it sets, fold through the whipped cream. Place an even amount of mixture into each mould and place in the refrigerator for a minimum of 4 hours.

To prepare the pastry, mix the honey and melted butter together and lightly warm on the stove. Prepare a baking sheet lined with silicon paper and preheat an oven to 160°C. In a bowl place the ready-made shredded pastry, the warmed butter and the honey mixture and mix well with your hands. Scatter the honey coated shredded pastry over the silicon paper. Spread it out to a thin layer. Bake for approximately 10 to 15 mins or until golden brown. Allow to cool before using.

Assemble
Remove the panna cottas from their moulds and invert into martini glasses. Peel back the clingfilm and top each panna cotta with a generous mixture of raspberries, currants and pistachio nuts. Sprinkle over the baked kataifi pastry, dust with icing sugar and serve.

POMEGRANATE MERINGUES WITH PISTACHIO GF

Donated by Thomasina Miers
@thomasinamiers

"Watching the civil war in Syria unfold has been desperate. I narrowly missed going on a wonderful food trip to Syria – which was an incredibly cool place to visit when I started working in food – and it is devastating to think of how many buildings have been ruined and lives torn apart since then. It is tragic to see a country of educated, hospitable, generous, warm and cultured people driven to starvation and homelessness. In supporting those people in need, this book is a wonderful thing."

Serves 6-8

4 medium good quality egg whites

210g caster sugar, preferably unrefined for the colour

3 tbsp pomegranate molasses

60g pistachios, finely chopped

1 large pomegranate

400ml double cream

This is a spectacular pudding of bewitching colours, all blushing meringues, vivid green pistachio dust and the sparkle of pomegranate jewels. I saw some green pistachio dust in a wonderful restaurant in Istanbul years ago and it stayed with me. You can go wild drizzling the whole thing with the pomegranate syrup – it is a lot of fun.

Preheat the oven to 100°C and line two baking trays with silicone sheets or parchment paper.

In a clean bowl whisk the egg whites with an electric whisk until you have stiff, stiff peaks. Now whisk in the sugar, little by little by little, followed by half the pomegranate syrup and a pinch of salt, fully incorporating the sugar with each addition until the whites are stiff again, shiny and voluminous – this takes about 10 mins.

With two teaspoons scoop high heaps of the mix onto the baking sheets, fluffing the tops into peaks. The meringue will do this pretty much automatically but, no matter how messy they are now, they will look beautiful once assembled. Dust each of the peaks with a sprinkling of the green pistachio nuts, saving half for the final plating. Bake in the oven for 2-3 hours, until the undersides are no longer sticky and peel away easily from the trays. Leave to cool in the turned off oven.

Meanwhile roll the pomegranate firmly along the work surface, pressing down so that you can feel the seeds 'popping' out. Cut the fruit in half over a bowl and tear open a piece at a time to release the seeds into the bowl, discarding the shell and white pith. Blitz half the seeds in a blender and sieve to get a beautiful red juice; keep both seeds and juice for later. Softly whip the cream until it is thick but still quite floppy and stir in the rest of the pomegranate molasses. Whisk the cream lightly with a wooden spoon until it just holds it shape – you can do this up to five hours ahead and store in the fridge.

Put everything together just before you are going to eat so that the meringue doesn't go soggy. Gather friends to help – it is great fun for everyone to get stuck in. Sandwich together the meringues with the cream and lay out on a large platter. Scatter with the pomegranate seeds and pistachios and splash with the brilliant red juice. Bring to the table and bask in glory.

DESSERTS

Photography by @tarafisherphoto
Styling by @rosieramsden

ORANGE BLOSSOM & PISTACHIO MERINGUE WITH CARDAMOM CREAM AND POMEGRANATE COULIS GF

Donated by Maria Bizri of Pomegranate Kitchen
@pomegranatekitchenhk

"I grew up walking the streets of Damascus, a place full of warmth and culture, depth and diversity and it's heartbreaking to see what is happening to Syria and its people. There will be a generation of children that have not known anything but refugee camps and war. For me, food is about culture and storytelling. I am grateful to have been asked to take part in this project and support the initiative while telling a story about a country that I love."

Makes 12 generous servings

For the meringue
600g caster sugar
300g egg-white
2.5 tsp orange blossom
1 tsp rose water
100g toasted pistachios, roughly chopped

For the cardamom cream
1.5 litre cream
2 tsp cardamom, dry roasted and very finely ground
½ cup sugar
zest of 2 lemons and 1 orange

For the pomegranate coulis
juice of 4 pomegranates
2 cups of fresh or frozen raspberries
zest of 1 lemon
¼ cup sugar

To garnish
pistachios
confit orange zest
pomegranate seeds

Growing up in Damascus, there was a particular type of raw meringue called Natef. It was eaten alongside a pistachio-filled shortcrust biscuit. You took the biscuit, dipped it in the Natef and ate it up. I remember it felt like I was dipping my biscuit into a little fluffy orange blossom flavoured cloud. I also love an Eton mess, so for this recipe I wanted to marry the two and the result was a pistachio filled orange blossom meringue with a light and fluffy cardamom infused cream and berry coulis.

For the meringue
Place the egg-white in a mixing bowl and beat on a medium speed for 6-8 mins. Gradually start adding your sugar very slowly allowing it to be fully dissolved in the egg-white mixture. Continue whisking for another 10-12 mins until the mixture is silky and shiny and the meringue forms stiff peaks.

Next add the orange blossom, rose water, chopped pistachio and fold.

Turn the oven temperature to 80°C and spoon meringues onto a lined baking tray. Use two large spoons one to scoop and one to push meringue mix onto the tray.

Place the meringue in the oven and cook for 3 hours, then turn the oven off and let the meringues cool with the oven.

For the cream
While the meringues are baking, place the cream in food processor on medium to high speed and whisk for 4-5 mins. Start adding the sugar bit by bit and whisk until it dissolves fully in the cream. Make sure not to over whip your cream as you want it fluffy yet ever so slightly runny.
Add the cardamom and zest of both the lemon and orange and mix until well combined - set aside.

For the coulis
Place the pomegranate juice, raspberries, sugar and lemon zest in a pot. Add 1 cup of water and bring to a boil, once boiled, let simmer for 10-12 mins. Turn off the heat and blend with a hand blender until nice and smooth.

Assembly
Drizzle your plate with the coulis and place the meringue in the middle. Top your meringue with cardamom cream, then more coulis. Cover with pomegranate seeds, chopped pistachios and confit orange zest (to confit orange zest, bring ¼ cup of sugar and ½ cup of water to a boil, add finely chopped orange skin/zest and cook for 4-5 mins. Let cool in the syrup. This can stay in an airtight container in the fridge for up to 4-6 weeks).

Photography by @petramgreening
Styling by @pomegranatekitchenhk

KETMER: PISTACHIO, CREAM AND ROSE BAKLAVA

Donated by Sarit Packer and Itamar Srulovich of Honey & Co.
@honeyandco

"If the Middle East is known for conflict and strife, it is also for known for great food traditions which stem from the friendly, hospitable nature of its people – an aspect that is sometimes overshadowed but should be celebrated, preferably with something sweet. Growing up, we would go to corner shops selling tray upon tray of sugary goods to a mixed clientele: Christians, Muslims, Jews, Druze, Bahá'í – we would share the same foods and we hope this book and initiative will remind us all that we come from one place and that we have more in common than differences."

Makes 6 individual pieces:

1 small pack of filo pastry
60g melted butter

For the filling (double the amounts if you want to serve with extra cream on the side)
100g mascarpone
100g double cream
zest of 1 lime
80g ground pistachio

For the syrup
100g sugar
50g water
1 tsp lime juice
1 tsp rose water

For the rhubarb
200g rhubarb
2 strips of orange skin
50g sugar
juice of 1 orange

Our food has always been inspired by our birthland [Israel]: rose water, orange blossom, honey and nuts are a great part of our cooking. Elaborate sweets made with crisp, syrup drenched pastry, fragrant flower water, sweet spices, fruit and nuts are a special feature of Middle Eastern cuisine. This version of Baklava is made with rich cream and pistachios and is best served with a sharp compote – strawberry or plum when in season, or as suggested here, rhubarb.

Mix the cream, mascarpone and lime zest together using a spoon until it thickens but doesn't whip.

Carefully open the filo pack – you will need 6 sheets. Lightly butter half a sheet and fold over lengthwise so that you get a double sheet rectangle. Spread a heaped tablespoon of the cream mix all over, sprinkle with a heaped tbsp of pistachios and very lightly roll to a loose snake, keeping plenty of air in the roll, then twist to create a snail shape tucking the end just under the snail to seal, place on a baking tray, repeat another 5 times and brush the top of all 6 generously with melted butter.

Heat the oven to 190°C with fan assist. Cut the rhubarb into 4 cm segments, place in a small roasting pan or oven safe frying pan and top with the sugar, orange strips and orange juice. Place in the oven and bake for 8 mins.

Place the ketmer in the oven and bake for 12-15 mins until golden all over. While in the oven, make the syrup by boiling the sugar and water, removing from the heat and adding the lime juice and rose water.

Once the ketmer are lovely and golden, remove from the oven, drizzle very generously with the syrup (traditionally you would use all of it, but I think start with just over half the amount and then decide whether to add more).

Serve with the roasted rhubarb and extra cream. Best eaten warm but still lovely at room temperature later in the day.

ALMOND, MAPLE & ROSE MAHALABI MILK PUDDING
GF, DF, V

Donated by Safia Shakarchi
@dearsafia

"Being involved in #BakeForSyria has been an amazing adventure. Using my sweet treats to give back to a region to which I owe a lot of who I am is a small but special contribution, which I feel lucky to make. A sweet tooth has no borders, and I hope that this book allows us to better understand that beautiful part of the world."

750ml almond milk
60g cornflour
60ml maple syrup, or to taste
1 tsp ground cardamom
3 tbsp rose water

To finish
slivered pistachios
edible rose petals
cardamom granola

Mahalabi was the first of many desserts my grandmother taught me to make. We would plan to eat it after dinner, but we'd always make two extra cups to have before then because obviously neither of us could wait that long! This version puts a contemporary twist on her recipe. The almond milk not only adds a lovely, sweet nuttiness to the pudding, but it also makes it dairy free, and the maple syrup means no refined sugar either. Whether made in one large dish or in individual cups, you'll always find mahalabi on the table at a Middle Eastern dinner party.

Place 650ml almond milk into a small saucepan along with the maple syrup and ground cardamom. Combine the remaining 100ml of almond milk with the cornflour in a mug to form a thick paste. Add this paste into the saucepan and bring the mixture to the boil, whisking gently and constantly to ensure it doesn't catch.

Reduce the heat slightly, add in the rose water and continue whisking until the mixture thickens to a custard-like consistency. Immediately pour into individual cups or a large dish, as is done traditionally. Set aside to come to room temperature and refrigerate until set (about 4 hours, ideally overnight).

When you're ready to serve, finish with your choice of toppings. Almost anything will work here – slivered pistachios are most traditional, but edible rose petals make a pretty finish and homemade granola adds a nice crunch too.

Photography by @KatieWilsonFoto
Styling by Safia Shakarchi
Portrait by Holly Wulff-Petersen

DATE & ESPRESSO ICE-CREAM GF

Donated by Kitty Travers of La Grotta
@lagrottaices

"During the late stages of being pregnant with my daughter I would head to the Syrian sweet shops on Edgware Road. There I could choose between crisp pastries dripping with syrup, fat dates tasting like butter fudge, stretchy hand-pounded mastic ice-cream rolled in pistachios and my favourite – huge cakes of crumbling, melting halva. Pure afternoon delight.

NB The factory which produced that halva no longer exists, a bleak reminder of one of the consequences of war on a wonderful culture."

Makes approx. 1 Litre or 10 scoops.

300ml whole milk
150ml double cream
50g coarsely ground freshly roasted coffee beans
pinch of sea salt
50g unrefined brown sugar
3 large egg yolks
60g medjool dates, pitted

This rather unusual method of cooking an ice cream base involves gently oven baking espresso-scented milk and cream with sticky dates to a set custard, before cooling, blending and churning. It's no exaggeration to say it transforms into the richest silkiest ice cream base you've ever tasted. Dates and coffee have a natural affinity and make a sophisticated, after-dinner pairing. The fruit's natural toffee sweetness means you use less sugar in the ice cream than you would normally need so its healthy too!

Preheat the oven to 120°C.

Heat the milk, cream and sea salt together in a heavy bottomed non-reactive pan. Bring to a simmer over a medium heat, whisking often to prevent scorching.

Once the liquid is hot and steaming, remove from the heat and whisk in the ground coffee. Cover the pan with a tightly fitting lid or cling film and set aside to steep for 15 mins.

Whisk the egg yolks and brown sugar together in a separate bowl to combine.

Pour the warm milk mix through a fine sieve or chinois to remove the coffee, over the yolks, whisking continuously.

Pour the custard into a shallow baking tray. Ideally around 12 inches by 9 inches. Add the pitted dates to the tray; try to submerge them in the thin coffee custard if possible.

Carefully transfer the tray to your oven, and bake very gently until just set in the middle but still wobbly (don't worry if the edges are a little more cooked) for between 20-25 mins depending on the depth of your pan.

Remove the custard from oven and scrape the mixture into a blender, whizz until very smooth and liquid again. Pour the custard into a clean container, then cool by setting in to a sink of iced water.

Once cool, refrigerate, covered, overnight.

The following day remove the custard from the fridge and blend the with a stick blender for a minute to re-liquify.

Pour the custard into an ice-cream machine and churn according to the machine's instructions until frozen and the texture of whipped cream.

Transfer the churned ice-cream into a suitable lidded container. Top with a piece of waxed paper to limit exposure to air, cover and freeze until ready to serve.

Photography by @CharlotteHuCo
Styling by @lily_vanilli_cake

HALVA & TOASTED PISTACHIO ICE CREAM GF

Donated by Yee Kwan
@yeekwanicecream

"Sharing my love of food is my passion and for me to have the opportunity to be involved with #CookForSyria and #BakeForSyria is very important to me. When I read stories about what innocent people have suffered during the civil war in Syria it is truly heartbreaking. Everyone deserves to live a peaceful and joyous life and for their children to have an education. I am grateful and love being involved in raising awareness for this worthwhile initiative."

Makes 1l

250ml whole milk
150g sugar
500ml double cream
6 large egg yolks (free range)
½ teaspoon salt
50g white sesame seeds (ground) or 50g tahini
50g pistachios
honey or cotton candy (optional, to serve)

This ice-cream recipe has a deliciously smoky and nutty flavour, topped with toasted pistachios and a drizzle of honey. I love sesame seeds because they are such a versatile ingredient and can be used in many savoury and sweet dishes. They are also popular in Chinese cuisine and my mother used to make yummy mocha balls filled with black sesame paste and roll them in toasted sesame seeds.

Lightly toast the white sesame seeds for 5 mins, until they are golden colour. Set aside to cool, using a spice grinder, grind them down to a fine powder. An easier and more convenient method is to use ready made tahini, but the aroma and flavour from the toasted sesame seeds will give you a more complex flavour and tastier ice cream!

Heat the milk, double cream, salt and sugar in a saucepan to 75°C.

Whisk the egg yolks in a large mixing bowl, and then slowly add the ice cream mix over the yolks, whisking quickly to ensure that the eggs don't scramble.

Add the ice cream base mix back into the saucepan and re-heat until the mix thickens and coats the back of a spoon.

Add the toasted sesame powder or tahini into the ice cream base mix.

Pour the ice cream base mix through a sieve and put the mixture into a large Ziploc bag and seal.

Put the Ziploc bag directly into the water bath to cool.

Pour the ice cream mix into your ice cream bowl / machine and freeze.

Once it is frozen down, put into the freezer to freeze further ready for serving.

Remove the pistachio nuts from the shells, carefully toast them and crush them in a pestle and mortar.

Scoop 2 balls of ice cream into a bowl, decorate with the pistachio nuts and drizzle with honey or some halva candy floss.

Photography by @KatieWilsonFoto
Styling by @lily_vanilli_cake
Portrait by Pete Hill

KATAIFI, HONEY AND WALNUT TRIFLE

Donated by Georgina Hayden
@georgiepuddingnpie

"I got involved in #BakeForSyria because I wanted to do what I could to help an amazing cause and because I really believe in the power of cooking to unite people. Whether it's a friendly dinner or making a cake for a bake sale, cooking can be such a healing and positive experience."

Serves 12-14

250g kataifi
75g butter
75g walnuts
8 tbsp honey
750g apples or pears
5 cloves
200g caster sugar
8 gelatine leaves
1l milk
4 egg yolks
4 tbsp cornflour
2 tsp orange blossom water
300ml double cream
250g Greek yoghurt

I initially made this decadent trifle over the christmas period, adorning it with gold leaf to make it more festive. However don't let that stop you: it's impressive any time of year and makes a fantastic dinner party pudding. My family are Greek Cypriot and many of our foods and ingredients are influenced by Syria and the Middle East. So many of the flavours are nostalgic to me, and the use of kataifi is something that is popular in both countries. You may have to seek it out – try any good international supermarket.

Preheat your oven to 200°C/ gas mark 6. Melt the butter in a small saucepan. Gently tease the kataifi apart and drape it all over the greased tin, patting it in lightly. Spoon the melted butter over the pastry and pop the tin in the oven for 15 mins. Meanwhile roughly chop 50g of the walnuts, then scatter over the kataifi. Return to the oven for a further 15 mins or until golden all over. Drizzle over 3 tablespoons of honey and leave to cool completely.

Peel the apples or pears and cut into 2cm wedges, cutting out the core. Place in a medium sized saucepan with the cloves, 140g caster sugar, 3 tablespoons of the honey and 800ml water. Add the lemon peel and place on a medium heat. Bring to the boil, then reduce to a simmer and poach for 10 mins until the fruit is just cooked through with a little bite. Remove from the syrup and leave to cool completely. Keep the syrup to one side.

Break the cooled kataifi into pieces and line the bottom of a 26cm diameter serving dish, pressing it to form a dense even layer. When the fruit is cooled lay them over the soaked kataifi. Measure out the poaching syrup, and top it up with water to make 800ml. Pour back into the pan to warm through. Soak the gelatine leaves in a bowl of water for 5 mins, then squeeze them and whisk into the warmed poaching syrup until totally dissolved. Leave to cool completely, then pour over the kataifi and poached fruits. Pop the dish in the fridge and leave for at least 4 hours, or until completely set.

When it is ready, make the custard layer. Fill your sink with a few inches of cold water. Heat the milk in a large saucepan over a low heat until warm. Meanwhile, whisk the egg yolks with the remaining 60g of caster sugar and the cornflour. Pour in a couple of ladlefuls of the warmed milk onto the eggs and quickly whisk it in. Pour the mixture into the pan of warmed milk and whisk constantly until thickened. Be careful it doesn't scramble. Pour the custard through a sieve into a large bowl, whisk in the orange blossom water and place into the cold water until it has cooled completely. When ready, pour it over the jelly layer and pop the dish back in the fridge to set.

When the trifle is ready whisk the double cream until you have soft peaks, then whisk in the yoghurt. Spoon over the custard and drizzle over the last 2 tablespoons of honey. Chop the remaining walnuts and scatter over the cream.

DESSERTS   Photography by @georgiepuddingnpie

SYRIAN ORANGE CAKE, FRESH YOGHURT, POMEGRANATE AND MINT

Donated by Juan Arbelaez
@juanalberleaz

"I think I was asked to be involved in this adventure partly because I come from a place that has suffered a lot. Colombia is a country that knows about hard times and I have lived all these experiences. I understand conflict and I want to try, through my actions, to make this world better."

Serves 8

The cake
250ml sunflower oil
1 cup of sugar
200g of greek yogurt
1 vanilla pod
11g baking powder
zest of 1 orange
4 eggs
1 pack of filo pastry

The syrup
2 cups of sugar
500ml water
250ml orange juice

To serve
fresh yogurt
1 grapefruit
1 pomegranate
few pistachios
fresh mint

I think this recipe is a good example of what Syrian cuisine is about. It's a dish to eat with your hands, walking down the street and sharing with people. For me, food is not only a matter of the actual dish – it's also about where you eat it, the way you eat it and people you share it with.

Cake recipe
Preheat oven to 170 °C.
Take the filo paste and cut into small pieces
In a bowl, put oil, sugar, baking powder, eggs, zest and vanilla and beat everything together.
Add the small pieces of filo paste into the mix.
Beat again to combine.
Add the Greek yogurt and blend just a little bit to combine evenly.
Blend everything until the sugar melts in the oil.
Put the mix into a baking dish and put in the oven

Bake for 30 minutes.

Syrup
Mix sugar, water and orange juice and heat to melt sugar.

Assembly
Remove dish from the oven and drizzle syrup all over.
Note: cake and syrup must not be at the same temperature. Either put the cold syrup on top of the hot cake or hot syrup on top of cold cake.

To serve
Add 2 tablespoons of fresh yogurt, some grapefruit segments and some pomegranate seeds.

Finish with some crushed pistachios and chopped mint.

Photography by @juanalberleaz

POMEGRANATE AND ROSE WATER SEMIFREDDO GF

Donated by Skye McAlpine
@skyemcalpine

"#CookforSyria is a celebration not just of Syrian cuisine, but of Syrian culture and of how food can bring us all together across the world. Since it started, #CookforSyria has raised over 500k to help the children in Syria have a future; I am hugely proud to be a part now of #BakeforSyria - let's raise another 500k!"

370ml double cream

2 eggs

4 egg yolks

75g sugar

1tsp rose water

140ml pomegranate juice

200g pomegranate seeds, and more for decoration

45g meringues

This Semifreddo is laced with crumbled white meringues and rose water, and tastes like a creamy Turkish Delight. I've added a dash of pomegranate juice, giving the cream that irresistibly soft pink colour and a few seeds for good measure too. I like the tartness against the rich cream, but I also love how they run through the pudding like shards of scarlet hued glass or semi precious stones.

Line a 20cm round cake tin with cling film, allowing a generous overhang on all sides and set to one side.

Whisk the cream until stiff and set to one side while you make the custard.

Crack the eggs and yolks into a heatproof bowl and pour in the sugar. Set the bowl over a pot of simmering water, and whisk the eggs vigorously with a handheld electric whisk for 4-5 mins until they become tick and creamy. Then take them off the heat and whisk for a further 4-5 mins until cool. Gently fold in the whipped cream. Pour in the rose water and fold in the pomegranate juice, little by little. Now the pomegranate seeds, and crumble in the meringues, then fold gently through. Cover with cling film and freeze overnight or until firm.

Before serving, stand at room temperature for 5-10 minutes, then turn out on to a plate and decorate with pomegranate seeds. Slice like a cake.

BAKED SAFFRON LEMONADE GF, DF

Donated by Missy Flynn
@missyflynn

"I'm stoked to be able to contribute to #CookforSyria even in the smallest way. I think we have so much power within the food and hospitality industry to highlight issues concerning conflicts and displacement, simply because we have understanding of food and its importance at the heart of communities. It's been amazing to see #CookForSyria and #BakeForSyria expand and remain a thoughtful, considered and pro-active effort to support those in need."

4 to 5 unwaxed lemons
500g caster sugar
pinch of saffron
ice cubes
sparkling water
fresh mint (to garnish)
lemon slivers (to garnish)
pomegranate seeds (to garnish)
honey or caster sugar

This recipe is a twist on a lemonade my friend Jack used to make at The Ten Bells. It came to me as I was thinking about low-waste ingredients that offer multiple dimensions of flavour, depending on how you treat them. I was inspired to use whole lemons by the preserved lemons common in Middle Eastern cuisine. We associate lemons with a sharp, citrus taste and often balance the sourness with sugar. Keeping the skin allows us to explore a third layer of flavour in bitterness, which I love in drinks like aperitifs or alongside desserts. Saffron adds a mesmerising colour and makes this baked lemonade more special. It can also be prepared in a jug to share!

Preheat oven to 150°C.

Take 4/5 unwaxed lemons and prick them a few times with a fork and remove the hard bit at the end where the stalk would have been. Place them on a baking tray, on top of a piece of baking paper or parchment.

Bake in the oven for forty-five mins to an hour depending on the size of the lemons. You'll know they are done when the skins turn a lovely golden colour and the lemons be all puffed up and juicy.

Take them out of the oven and cover with tin foil to cool - this cools them slowly and keeps them wrapped in moisture so they stay nice and juicy. Meanwhile, stir 500g of caster sugar into 500ml boiled water until it dissolves. Whilst it's still warm stir in a pinch of saffron.

Once the lemons are at room temperature, chop them up into chunks, ideally in the baking tray so you can keep hold of any juice or pulp that might otherwise get lost.

Blend these chunks, skin and all with the saffron sugar syrup. It's fine to leave little chunks of skin in there, but if you prefer a smoother drink blend until it's a more like a fruit purée or compote. If you like your drinks on the sweeter side, you should now taste and add more caster sugar or a touch of honey to taste.

To assemble the drink, measure 100ml of the lemon mix and add ice cubes, mix vigorously, and top up with sparkling water, garnishing with fresh mint, lemon slices, pomegranate seeds or saffron if you are feeling fancy.

Serve with a long spoon so your guests can mix as they drink.

DESSERTS

Photography by @CharlotteHuCo
Styling by @lily_vanilli_cake

SPECIAL THANKS

We are so grateful to everyone who has supported the #CookForSyria and #BakeForSyria initiatives, it is awe-inspiring to watch how much it has grown and how many people it resonates with, so thank you to everyone who has helped, contributed, bought a book or attended one of the events.

Special thanks goes to all the chefs, bakers and food writers who donated their time and recipes to the project. It has been so exciting seeing people from all over the world respond to the brief and create a dish that celebrated Syrian cuisine for them.

Huge thanks also to the photographers - Katie Wilson, Charlotte Hu (London) and Nikki To (in Australia) who helped source props, ran around town getting shots from restaurants or endured long photoshoots with an average of 40 shots a day. Safia Shakarchi who helped with styling and coordinating the shoot days. It was a joy to work with you.

Thank you to the magnificent (co-founder of #CookForSyria) Gemma Bell and her team, in particular Alice Grier and Raffaela Holzapfel, Gemma Bell and Company for managing the PR for the project and spreading the word, you always nail it Gemma.

The talented and generous Sam Thompson of Shrinkpad Designs who worked on all the design for the book and did so with grace and speed.

Harry Strawson who gave so much of his time, patience and diligence to editing the book.

Melissa Hemsley, Imad Alarnab, Laura Jackson, Henrietta Inman, Justin Gellatly, Pophams Bakery and Safia Shakarchi (again) for always stepping up and volunteering to help with every pop-up event or project, no matter how crazy or last minute, it is so incredibly generous. Also a huge thank you to everyone involved in the #CookForSyria Christmas pop-up in Seven Dials.

The Unicef NEXTGen committee – Linda Blank, operations and finance extraordinaire; Noura Al-Maashouq and Layla Yarjani for making things happen and Hortense Decaux and the Codi team for building a beautiful website. Also a big thank you to the wider committee for their patience and support when things needed to be turned around faster than the speed of light.

Monica Tanouye, Charlotte Westbrook and Thomas Sayers from Unicef for help with communication, guidance and help building this into a global campaign.

The wonderful people at Rye Studios who let us use their beautiful space for the shoot days

Sam Neill at Pro Lighting London who kindly donated lighting for the shoot days.

Piers Herron at Backgrounds Prop Hire who lent us props and backdrops for the shoots.

Pat Nourse from Gourmet Traveller and Jeanine Bribosia from Cru Media for all their incredible support in Australia.

Felicity Spector for her contributions and endless backing.

Paula Hagan who helped collate the content.

Dorcas Brown who helped at the final hour.

Ana from Kana London who lent us her beautiful ceramics.

Carla from Still Life Flowers who kindly donated flowers for the shoot days.

Vicki Baker of Bang Bang events and Lucy McGarry for helping pull together the first #BakeForSyria events.

Rupert Harbour, who got this recipe book into stores around the nation and beyond.

Dora Miller set design for the pink walls.

Photo assistants. Kerimcan Goren, Magda Siwicka, Jake Webber, Jeanette Dear.

Our dear friends and family for their ongoing support throughout the whole journey.

And finally, we would like to thank all of you around the world who are getting involved, and sharing your experiences, be it in your home, restaurant or even office. We hope that through these recipes, many others will start and continue to #CookForSyria or #BakeForSyria.

INDEX

INDEX

CONTRIBUTORS

INDEX

Published in 2018 by SUITCASE Media International Ltd
Text © SUITCASE Media International Ltd
Photography by Charlotte Hu, Katie Wilson and Nikki To

Additional photos by: Alan Keohane, Bonnie Savage, Chris Terry, Gabrielle
Motola, Helen Cathcart, Helena Dolby, Holly Farrier, Holly Wulff-Petersen, Issy
Croker, Izy Hossack, Jamie Oliver Enterprises Limited, Joe Woodhouse, John
Dale, Jonathan Lovekin, Kate Whitaker, Katie Musgrave, Lucy McNally, Mikkel
Vang, Murrindie Frew, Nassima Rothacker, Nick Hopper, Nicolas Villion, Patricia
Niven, Pete Hill, Sarah Lemanski, Sarah Malcolm, Sophia Spring, Stephanie de
Goeijen, Sukaina Rajabali, Tara Fisher

A CIP catalogue record for this title is available from the British Library Forest
Stewardship Council

Curator and founder #BakeForSyria: Lily Vanilli
Editor: Harry Strawson
Designer: Sam Thompson - Shrinkpad.com
Photographers: Charlotte Hu, Katie Wilson and Nikki To
Food stylist: Lily Vanilli, with help from Safia Shakarchi
Founders #CookForSyria: Clerkenwell Boy, Serena Guen and Gemma Bell

Printed and bound in the UK by CPI Colour ISBN 978-1-5272-2219-63
Copyright ©SUITCASE Media International Ltd All rights reserved

All profits from this book will support children affected by the crisis in Syria
through Unicef Next Generation London, a fundraising group of Unicef UK.
Unicef UK registered charity 1072612 (England and Wales) and SC 043677
(Scotland). CookForSyria.com